Thwarting Enemies at Home and Abroad

Other Intelligence Titles from
Georgetown University Press

Analyzing Intelligence: Origins, Obstacles, and Innovations
Roger Z. George and James B. Bruce, Editors

Transforming U.S. Intelligence
Jennifer E. Sims and Burton Gerber, Editors

Thwarting Enemies

at Home and Abroad

How to Be a
Counterintelligence
Officer

William R. Johnson

Foreword by William Hood

Georgetown University Press ◈ Washington, D.C.

Georgetown University Press,
Washington, D.C.
www.press.georgetown.edu

Library of Congress Cataloging-in-Publication Data

Johnson, William R., d. 2005.
   Thwarting enemies at home and abroad: how to be a
counterintelligence officer /
William R. Johnson ; foreword by William Hood.
       p. cm.
   Originally published: Bethesda, Md. : Stone Trail Press, c1987.
   Includes bibliographical references and index.
   ISBN 978-1-58901-255-4 (pbk. : alk. paper)
   1. Intelligence service. I. Title.
   UB250.J64 2008
   355.3'432—dc22
       2008029498

This book is printed on acid-free paper
meeting the requirements of the American
National Standard for Permanence in Paper
for Printed Library Materials.

15 14 13 12   9 8 7 6 5 4

Printed in the United States of America

Contents

Publisher's Note

The original 1987 edition of *Thwarting Enemies at Home and Abroad* has been out of print for many years, but it has continued to be sought after by professionals, scholars, and others interested in the real world of intelligence. Georgetown University Press has republished this book to make sure that William R. Johnson's seasoned wisdom about the principles and tactics of counterintelligence is widely available once again.

We have republished the original text in full and unaltered except for corrections for grammar and punctuation that naturally slip through in an original edition. We also added a new foreword to provide perspective on the book and the author's career. The book has not been revised to account for changes in technology or world affairs for two main reasons. First, the main point of the book is to teach readers how to think about counterintelligence, and these basic principles carry through from era to era. Updates to account for current events and the latest gadgetry would have short-term benefit but would be dated once again within a few years. Second, the author passed away before republication was planned, so we elected not to attempt revisions that could not be approved by the author.

Foreword

Espionage is most deftly defined as the theft of secrets. In contrast, counterintelligence is a grab bag of responsibilities ranging from keeping secrets beyond the grasp of hostile spies, the curious passerby, and even journalists, to the study of foreign intelligence agencies and individuals most likely to be involved in espionage.

Counterespionage is another, and surely more sensitive, highest-level element of counterintelligence. It involves the use of captured or detected foreign agents to deceive and mislead their sponsors. The best-known example of contemporary counterespionage is the Allied use of captured German spies operating under Allied control to report the "intelligence" that helped keep Hitler convinced that the actual invasion landings on the Normandy beaches in World War II were but a feint to cover the "real" landings many miles to the north of the actual invasion.

As a captain and battalion intelligence officer in the U.S. Second Infantry Division, William R. Johnson fought his way across the Normandy beaches on June 6, 1944. By May 1945, he was in newly liberated Pilsen, Czechoslovakia.

After the war and a spell of postgraduate study and teaching, Bill asked an old friend with whom he had helped edit and publish *Furioso* at Yale—a much-respected undergraduate literary magazine that had attracted T. S. Eliot's attention—if there might be a job at the Central Intelligence Agency (CIA).

"Hell, yes," Jim Angleton said. At the time, Angleton was chief of CIA's counterintelligence staff.

Bill's first assignments—in Europe—gave him a front-row seat and role in some of the most successful CIA operations of the early Cold War period. When Heinz Felfe, a ranking officer in the newly established West German intelligence service, first fell under suspicion, Bill, an ardent skier and alpinist, donned his lederhosen and on his own initiative scouted the isolated Bavarian chalet that Felfe claimed to have bought with funds supplied by an alleged aunt in the United States.

Sure enough, there was the chalet, a tidy new construction, complete with a large color TV set. At the time, color TV was still an expensive luxury for any civil servant in Germany. The notion that a middle-level civil service officer could build a posh weekend getaway, and furnish it with such a costly item, was one of the convincing bits of evidence that led to the arrest and conviction of Felfe and a confederate.

After a dozen years in the vital European counterintelligence field, Bill's next posting took him back to Washington and a senior assignment managing CIA's Far Eastern counterintelligence operations from 1960 until his transfer to Saigon in 1973. This was an important breakthrough. Many of the senior CIA personnel involved with counterintelligence had got their start in World War II as members of X-2, the counterintelligence branch of General William Donovan's Office of Strategic Services (OSS). X-2 personnel worked closely—often hand in hand—with the experienced counterintelligence staff of their British colleagues in Europe and the Near East. The work involved apprehending German agents and directing their subsequent role in the deception of the Nazi intelligence services. X-2 played a much lesser role in the Pacific theater of operations.

During World War II, General Douglas MacArthur had refused to allow any significant OSS activity in the area under his command. The isolated exceptions to this *ukase* were largely restricted to occasional paramilitary activity behind Japanese lines, with little need for the counterespionage support that marked the strategic operations in Europe and the Near East. Counterintelligence also figured much less prominently in the OSS's Far Eastern activity than in Europe. Bill Johnson's 1960 assignment to CIA's Far Eastern division introduced a new level of CIA experience for that region. He remained in this position until 1973, when he was assigned to a senior command post in Saigon. He remained in Saigon until the evacuation of the U.S. Embassy and CIA station in 1975.

An incidental fact: Various allegations have been floated alleging that CIA abandoned much of its classified file material when evacuating Saigon. In truth, the only CIA documents that were not destroyed were some of those left in the liaison offices of the South Vietnamese intelligence services.

For some time after his retirement, Bill and his wife, Patricia, also a retired CIA veteran, remained in close social contact with their many Vietnamese friends in the Washington area. After moving to Colorado, Bill created a series of lectures on intelligence in government that is an important element of the University of Colorado's Conference on World Affairs.

Thwarting Enemies at Home and Abroad is a unique study and handbook on counterintelligence and counterespionage. It is well recognized as such and thus has been used in many university-level courses in the United States and abroad.

William Hood
Former CIA officer and author of
*Mole: The True Story of the First
Russian Spy to Become an
American Counterspy*

Introduction

I have written this book for people who want to know what counterintelligence is, not what it ought to be, and for people who may be interested in it as a trade or profession. The book is about what professional intelligence officers call "tradecraft," specifically the craft used in the trade of counterintelligence. It is not about politics, policy, communism, anticommunism, justice in the developing world, human rights, or religion, although these affect the trade of counterintelligence just as they do the trades of stockbroking, oil exploration, and journalism. They will be mentioned occasionally, and my concerns about them will be evident, but only as they are elements of the environment in which counterintelligence functions.

My thirty-odd years working in counterintelligence have all been spent as an American official, but I have worked much of that time with the counterintelligence officers of other countries. I believe that this book will be useful to readers not only in the United States but also in other countries allied with the United States and in some nonallied and nonhostile nations where espionage and terrorism occur.

To illustrate various points, I have cited many actual cases. Some of these have been written about publicly elsewhere, with varying degrees of accuracy, and some have not. Those that have not yet come to the attention of journalists, historians, or writers of fictional documentaries I have altered (in counterintelligence jargon, "sanitized") by changing names, dates, and places. I have done this to protect myself and to protect what American law calls "sources and methods" from hostile action. I have made some changes and deleted some material at the request of the U.S. Central Intelligence Agency, which has reviewed the contents patiently, promptly, and thoughtfully. What I know about the spy business I learned as an official under oath to my government, and therefore what facts I know about the spy business are the government's property, not mine. The *opinions* are my own, and the Central Intelligence Agency neither endorses nor condemns them.

WHAT IS COUNTERINTELLIGENCE?

People like to confuse counterintelligence (CI) with security. In practice, the two are related but not identical. Put it this way: Security is an essential part of all intelligence work, including CI.

So we have physical security—the fences around buildings, the badges people wear, the safes and the officers who regularly inspect them after hours to make sure they are locked and nothing is left out of them that should be locked up, the burn bags, the guard posts, the closed-circuit TV monitors, the coded telephone circuits to prevent eavesdropping—and a lot more. They keep out burglars and help prevent accidental or absentminded losses of information.

Then we have personnel security—background investigations of candidates for employment, periodic reinvestigation of employees—and more.

Finally, and especially in the intelligence business, we have operational security. This boils down to keeping your mouth shut, guarding secrets, both yours and your government's, and not letting anybody get into position to blackmail you. One more thing, the most important: Operational security requires adherence to the Law of Need-to-Know: Only persons who need to know a piece of sensitive information can have access to it. Incidentally, this law promotes efficiency by reducing paper handling.

Operational security is a way of life in all secret activity, whether it be CI, counterespionage (CE), espionage, adultery, or poker. It is to these activities what style is to a writer, an athlete, or a musician, but it is not itself a work, a game, or a performance. Like all security, its purpose is prophylactic: It excludes toxic and infectious organisms.

So much for security. What is different about CI?

Just what the name says: It is aimed against intelligence, against active, hostile intelligence, against enemy spies. And it is itself active, not passive.

CI uses a number of techniques, mostly various kinds of detection, investigation, and research. Ultimately, it uses the various techniques of CE. All its techniques are aimed at frustrating the active efforts of alien conspiratorial organizations to acquire secret or sensitive information belonging to the government that employs you.

Some people—journalists, politicians, novelists, and even some professionals—confuse CE with its parent, CI. The British tend to use "CE" to include "CI"—the opposite of the way this book will use the terms. Some lazy officers in the U.S. Central Intelligence Agency (CIA) simply say "CI/CE," but that is cheating. For the purposes of this book, CE is the branch of CI that penetrates and manipulates any alien spy apparatus. It is not only active; it is aggressive.

So the special thing about CE is manipulation. That is the final goal of all CI.

To look at it another way, remember that CE is a branch of espionage, and that espionage is theft. Espionage is stealing information and thereby breaking a law—the other person's law. If that person didn't have a law against you stealing it, it wouldn't be espionage. Nothing enfuriates a professional espionage officer more than to be told that her job is gathering information, as if she were a little girl in a pinafore gathering nuts in May, or a journalist. She steals information—carefully, selectively, secretly—using an apparatus of agents who are secretly recruited, trained, tested, monitored, and protected.

CE is also theft of information by use of an apparatus of agents. The difference is that when you steal a military secret from some country's air force or army, or a political secret from some country's foreign office, you call it espionage. When you steal it from an intelligence service, it is CE. And, along with the British and the American services, you may call that person you recruit, train, protect, pay, and supervise to steal a secret from a foreign government an "agent." If you are stealing from the former Soviet KGB (Komitet Gosudarstvennoy Bezopastnosti, Committee on State Security), the Swiss national police, or the Palestinian Liberation Organization, you have to call him or her a "penetration" ("mole"). Either way, he or she is a spy spying on a ("conspiratorial") spy service, and the information he or she steals will be used to manipulate that service.

Later in the book, we'll be talking about the techniques of CI, the tools of the trade:

- The support apparatus
- Interrogation
- Surveillance, and physical and technical double agents
- Penetrations (moles)
- Defectors
- Liaison
- Collating files

These are all used together for CI, for some special tasks like counterterrorism, and for the most important job that CI is called on to do: strategic deception.

WHO GOES INTO
COUNTERINTELLIGENCE, AND WHY?

In our time every country—large or small; communist or non-communist; aligned or nonaligned; developed, undeveloped, or developing—must conduct counterintelligence. In some countries CI is a major industry, in others it is a sideline of the local police, but it goes on everywhere because no country is exempt from espionage. In places like Burkina Faso, Paraguay, and Luxembourg, spies ply their trade, not against the local government but against other countries and against each other. Switzerland and Austria are not notorious spy centers because they have important secrets of their own, but because they are convenient places to run espionage operations.

The result of this situation of international espionage is an "International Counterintelligence Corps," an unofficial fraternity whose members do the same jobs and use the same tools, whatever language they speak and whatever flag they salute when their national anthem is played. There is no official Inter-CI like Interpol, but unofficially there is a comfortable cooperation among CI services. During the Cold War, the anti-Soviet services worked together in ad hoc arrangements. The Soviet Bloc services worked under the direct control of the KGB. And the neutrals picked and chose.

WHAT IS PECULIAR ABOUT CI OFFICERS?

An old hand comes to know that both within his own and in other CI services, professionals have traits in common, and they fall into three groups. The first is the *positive intelligence analyst*—give her a piece of paper with sentences of information on it, and she will immediately do three things:

1. Check it for accuracy.
2. Evaluate its place in the context of her own knowledge of its subject matter.
3. Try to exploit it for the production of a finished report or study that can be disseminated to decision makers at some level, the higher the better.

The second is the *espionage case officer*—give the same piece of paper to a case officer who runs agents to collect military or political or economic intelligence. He will also do three things, but they are different things:

1. Examine it to identify its source.
2. Attempt to learn or guess the author's motive for promulgating it.
3. Grope for a way of using it to influence somebody, usually a prospective agent.

The third is the *CI officer*. The CI officer's actions are a combination of those of the two other types of officers:

1. Like the intelligence analyst, the CI officer will try to exploit it by incorporating it into the context of her own knowledge, not for a "dissem" (disseminated finished intelligence report)

but for her growing and changing working files (see chapters 16 and 17). The "positive" intelligence—military, political, economic—is not of interest, except insofar as it may be deception or fabrication, and thus may point toward a CI target.

2. Like the espionage case officer, the CI officer will grope for a way to use the report to influence somebody, not to produce further espionage operations but to recruit a double agent or a penetration. If the report appears to be fabricated, he will intensify his investigation of the source, because that source is a point at which the enemy can be engaged. *Note:* Positive intelligence reports are normally in two parts, one containing the information, the other identifying the source by some sort of code. The part that gives the code name of the source is not disseminated to consumers. In those "conglomerate" services that conduct both espionage and CI, it is one of the jobs of the CI shop to maintain a continuous investigation of agents to detect those who have been mounted against the service (the agents provocateurs) or who have been uncovered and "turned" (doubled back) by an adversary.

3. Unlike either of his or her colleagues, the CI officer will wring the report dry of all information on persons, and incorporate that information into the file system.

Obviously, these distinctions are arbitrary. In practice—especially in conglomerate services like the U.S. Central Intelligence Agency, the British Secret Intelligence Service, and the

German Bundesnachrichtendienst—an officer must shift from one discipline to another and must often wear several hats at once—espionage case officer until lunch, intelligence analyst until dinner, and CI officer until bedtime. In these services individual officers tend to suffer a little from schizophrenia, which they alleviate by adopting one or another discipline as their specialty. The assignment of officers who are "CI oriented" to supervisory positions over units with heavy espionage burdens has been found to improve the quality of espionage production. Conversely, "production-oriented" supervisors often improve the efficiency of CI units they command. In the conglomerate services, all officers must be generalists, that is, a mixture of the three types we have been discussing, with an orientation toward one of the three.

CI TRAITS: DO YOU HAVE THEM?

Newcomers to the CI trade, and those thinking of joining it, may ponder some of the following traits.

Curiosity

It goes without saying that the kind of person to whom a job is only a job—a crank to be turned, a procedure to be followed, a day to be gotten through—will not want a job in the CI business, nor be wanted there. CI officers must have a special kind of curiosity, the kind that focuses on the material at hand and then ranges beyond it to adjacent areas. Even the beginner starting out as a file clerk must be curious about what he or she is filing and about the filing system itself. The venerable principle of operational security that a person should only have knowledge of what he needs to know is not violated by professional curiosity on the part of CI officers. Proper compartmentation, itself not possible without curiosity on the part of those who arrange it, keeps discipline.

Pattern Recognition

Cousin to curiosity is the habit of mind that looks for patterns, analogies, and parallels. The simplest form of pattern is what criminal police call modus operandi—"method of working"—the work habits of a particular criminal. The bank robber who twice wears a ski mask and twice points his weapon at the teller's head rather than body, then both times backs out of the bank, rather than running, has set a pattern that helps identify him.

In CI work, the patterns are more complex. If the enemy case officer tells your double agent that his appraisals of the crisis in Sri Lanka are highly valued by the center in Moscow, Prague, or Havana and that the service has just promoted him to colonel, you know that your double agent is being developed not as a writer of appraisals but as a support agent. His next requirement may well be to take a little trip to a region denied to the enemy case officer, where he is to empty a dead drop. How do you know this? Because you know the pattern: The Soviets, Czechs, or Cubans habitually flatter their agents and ease their agents' conscience and keep their agents busy by having them write "appraisals," which they then chuck in the burn bag while waiting for the time when a dead drop in Ouagadougou, El Arish, or Albuquerque has to be serviced by somebody who is not under suspicion and has a "cover" (an innocent reason) for traveling there. Or perhaps your double will be asked to introduce the enemy case officer to a friend, somebody with access to an intelligence target or to another friend with such access. The enemy case officer may suggest an innocent lunch at which she will be introduced under the false name she is already using with your double. She will suggest the lunch, of course, only as a minor, incidental favor in no way concerned with the important appraisals your double is writing about Sri Lanka.

Patterns are the name of the game when working against illegals (agents documented as nationals of a Western country, often having actual former Soviet Union country or satellite citizenship). During one period of the Cold War, a number of ostensible Canadians were uncovered as Soviet agents. Thus the Russian KGB officer Kolon Molodiy used the identity of a dead Canadian named Gordon Arnold Lonsdale, and another illegal used the identity of a Canadian who was still alive but had been judged never likely to apply for a passport. The KGB illegal support apparatus, using its own support agents, had formed a pattern of researching birth and death records in Canada (and Finland, New Zealand, South Africa, and elsewhere) in order to acquire birth certificates and thereby passports to alter and issue to illegals. When the pattern became clear to Western CI officers, a number of Soviet illegals were brought to book and a number of others were hastily recalled by the KGB and the GRU (Glavnoe Razvedovatel'noe Upravlenie, Soviet Military Intelligence Service).

Sensitivity to pattern is essential in detecting deception. The first pattern to look for in any case where your service seems to be having a great intelligence success is the success itself. Remember that the basic principle underlying deception is to tell your target what he wants to believe. If you have a success on your hands, look at it carefully: Is it telling you what you want to believe, or what is logical and probable? There is always a difference. Samson wanted to believe that Delilah loved him, when simple logic and knowledge of the Philistine pattern of behavior would have told him that she was after his scalp. Too late he found himself eyeless in Gaza, at the mill with slaves. Which shows that the history of CI goes back a long way, and the principles do not change.

At first glance, catching spies and studying English poetry do not seem to be closely related, but they have one thing in common: Both, when competently done, are based on recognizing patterns. It is no accident that some of the most effective British and American CI officers in World War II were drafted into that war from positions as critics of English literature. They had been trained to look for multiple meanings, to examine the assumptions hidden in words and phrases, and to grasp the whole structure of a poem or a play, not just the superficial plot or statement. So the multiple meanings, the hidden assumptions, and the larger pattern of a CI case were grist for their mill. I do not require my young CI officers to be able to discuss the complexities of a Shakespeare play, but if I catch them studying Brooks and Warren's *Understanding Poetry*, I do not instantly send them off to the firing range. I tell them to go read Cleanth Brooks on "the language of paradox," because CI is the act of paradox.

Interest in People

A physician who does not like to deal with patients face to face had better become a radiologist, forensic pathologist, or researcher. So a CI officer who shrinks from face-to-face contact with people had better stick to supporting the case officers from the safety of a desk. He or she must forswear the active part of CI—interrogation, field investigation, running double agents—and be forever subordinate, with no disgrace, to the officer in the field, the one who meets people, handles people, manipulates people.

The CI officer in the field, if he only pushes doorbells (please, Ma'am, just give me the facts), must have that quality that salespeople and priests have: a sympathetic interest in people and an incentive to manipulate them, like a priest to make them see the light and like a salesperson to make them buy his product. Without that quality, he should stay at the desk with the files. But that quality alone is not enough—in fact, alone, it is disastrous to a CI officer. He must also have the other traits described here.

The case officer in the field must interview strangers, manage surveillance teams, handle double agents, conduct interrogations, run (if she's lucky) penetrations, handle (if she's lucky) defectors—in other words, deal with people. And she must do this within the discipline of CI analysis and all that stuff about files.

Skepticism

Remember, newcomer to the CI business and old-timer as well, you are being paid to be lied to. The lies will come out of the mouths of your contacts and they will be on the paper you work from. Your job is to suppress your indignation and sort out the patterns. The more plausible something appears, the more suspicious you must be. I do hope you have a sense of humor about it all.

Patience

Mix together all the traits described above and they add up to patience. If your temper is short, learn to curb it. Experience will bring a kind of boredom, and you will think that you can never again be surprised. Then you will be surprised, and again surprised, until finally you will become bored with being surprised. You will then be a seasoned, and patient, CI officer. Begin to cultivate the virtue of patience as soon as possible. It will protect you from peptic ulcer, coronary attacks, hypertension, and alcoholism.

Nerve

In the CI business there are times when you have to act without adequate knowledge of your situation. In that respect, the CI business is a little like any combat situation in wartime. Sometimes, as in combat, the conditions are hazardous and require physical courage. Usually the hazards are merely bureaucratic. But they require a willingness to accept responsibility, to act quickly, and to face the consequences if you guess wrong. Nerve is needed at every point, whether in analyzing a case in the shelter of a file room or meeting a prospective penetration agent on enemy turf. We do not want cowboys in the CI business, but we have to have people who will make their own decisions and stick up for them afterward.

CONFLICTING GOALS: LAW ENFORCEMENT VERSUS MANIPULATION

Outside the Commonwealth (and Germany), most countries assign counterintelligence to their police organs. The reason is obvious: Espionage, sabotage, and terrorism are crimes, and crimes are the problem of the police.

The British make it more complicated. They give the job of engaging hostile services to a separate organ, which has no powers of arrest. This outfit is still called MI5 by the press, although its members call it the Security Service. They give the job of prosecuting intelligence crime to a Special Branch of the police, but they enjoin that branch from using such techniques of counterespionage as double agentry and penetration.

Members of the Commonwealth—for example, Australia, Canada, and New Zealand—use the British system. So do many former British colonies like Malaysia and Singapore, and so does Germany. In Australia, for example, the Security Service is confusingly called the Australian Security Intelligence Organization (ASIO), while in Germany it is jaw-breakingly called the Federal Office for Protection of the Constitution (Bundesamt für Verfassungsschutz, BfV). The BfV's counterpart "special branch" is the Security Group (Sicherungsgruppe,

SG) within the German Federal Criminal Police (Bundeskriminalamt, BKA).

None of these "internal" services is to be confused with the "external" services that operate beyond the borders of their countries—for example, the British Secret Intelligence Service (SIS), the Australian SIS (ASIS), and the German Bundesnachrichtendienst at home—but they all conduct both espionage and CI abroad, where by the nature of things they have no arrest powers. Their function is the same as that of the American CIA and the "external" services of most other noncommunist countries.

In the United States, as in most other of the non-British, noncommunist countries, the national police organ enforces laws against espionage as well as other federal laws. So the separation of prosecution from counterespionage has to exist within the Federal Bureau of Investigation (FBI), just as it exists, for example, within the Austrian State Police or the Thai National Police. This makes for some factionalism; it also makes for mutual education.

COPS WITH A CI JOB

If your job is enforcing the law, you use the machinery of the law. That means that your procedures are designed to detect crime, assemble evidence about it, and use that evidence in a fair trial to convict a criminal. You may have informants and stool pigeons who give you information about crime, and you may make arrangements to help these people avoid punishment in exchange for their information, but basically your aim is to get convictions in court.

For the law enforcement officer, the manipulation of criminals to damage a gang to which they belong is part of the job, but the damage he or she hopes to inflict is what a judge will sentence other members of the gang to after a jury has found them guilty of a crime. When the crime is armed robbery, embezzlement, or illegal gambling, these procedures are appropriate. When the crime is espionage, sabotage, or a terrorist murder, your life as a law enforcement officer takes on another dimension. Why? Because the conviction and judicial punishment of a spy may not be a useful goal for your government. Nor will the conviction and judicial punishment of a spy's organization be practical—for example, during the Cold War you could not indict the KGB in a court of law, or if you could have, you'd have played hell trying to bring the director of the KGB into court. The analogy between a foreign espionage service and a criminal gang is temptingly simple to the law enforcer, but if he applies it literally, he will have a lousy CI program.

If your organization is set up primarily for law enforcement, its procedures will influence, and sometimes dominate, your work—even if you keep thinking of your long-term objective of manipulating the alien intelligence service. The problem will be the manner in which you collect, file, and collate information. Pressure will be on you to assemble evidence, and to collect only that information that will support, lead to, or constitute evidence, the kind that can be sworn to by a firmly identified witness, or that can be laid on the clerk's table like a pistol or knife.

The trouble is that in CI, sources cannot be identified in open court without ceasing to be sources. And documentary evidence, whether laid on the clerk's table or only exposed in the discovery process of a trial, can destroy the usefulness of its sources.

SPYMASTERS WITH A CI JOB

Suppose your job is in a service that has no arrest powers. You will tend to view any form of "executive action" (which simply means arrest and trial) as a failure of your CI program.

But wait. The last time you detected a spy and went to recruit him as a double agent, how did you persuade him to cooperate? You probably gave him a choice between cooperating and being arrested. To be more credible, you may have even taken a police officer along.

Wait again. What about that case where you had learned that the old Hungarian State Security Service (AVH, the Hungarian equivalent of the KGB) knew that their agent had been doubled and was about to withdraw his handler? You made a try at recruiting the handler, taking your friendly police officer with you, and when the handler told you to go to hell, the police officer arrested him. Where, now asks the police officer, is your evidence for our prosecution?

And what about the case where your Department of State or Foreign Office ruled that a public trial was required as part of a diplomatic program? (This will happen often.) You saluted and went to work turning your CI information into evidence, trying to protect your sources and methods as best you could while working closely with the prosecutors.

So don't get to feeling all dedicated and superior because your primary job is CI, not law enforcement. You are not above the law.

COPS AND SPYMASTERS, MINGLE AND MERGE!

In the United States, the National Security Act of 1947 defined the charters of CIA and the FBI. The FBI, operating within the nation's boundaries, had investigative and arrest powers and a set of procedures that were meant to lead, through collection of evidence, to prosecutions in a federal court. CIA, chartered to work overseas with no power of arrest, had (from its predecessor agencies—the COI, OSS, SSU, and CIG) a set of procedures designed to engage hostile services through investigation, double agent operations, the use of defectors, and the insertion of penetrations (moles), but not to arrest anybody.

Alas for the comfort of those of us in both services, the separation of authority and responsibility that was so neatly set out in the National Security Act was in practice messy. Under the act, CIA passed to the FBI information acquired abroad on U.S. citizens and on foreign officials stationed in the United States. The FBI found much of this information difficult to handle, because CIA usually did not identify sources and it was all mostly "background"—not usable under rules of evidence.

In turn, the FBI, as required under the National Security Act, passed to CIA information on foreigners residing in the United States, when those foreigners went abroad. But CIA found this information cursory and often not pertinent. It seemed to suffer from a lack of curiosity about activities that were not in themselves crimes but that were part of a subject's operational work. The FBI also seemed not to care about the big picture—the shape of enemy espionage around the world, the structure of the KGB or its satellites.

The crunch came, repeatedly, when a double agent or penetration who had been developed abroad by CIA was transferred to the States and came under FBI jurisdiction. The difference in the attitude of his new handlers, the lack of interest in enemy requirements, the perfunctory or diffident attention to clearing and providing information for passage to the enemy—these all bewildered and discouraged the doubles. I remember one such case in which the double had been transferred from Europe, where he was used to having his reporting on enemy contacts receive exhaustive attention from his American handler. He found that his FBI handler seemed interested only in whether he had noticed the odometer reading on the car in which he met his enemy handler. His main function, he gathered, was to serve as a check on the FBI's surveillance of the enemy officer.

He disobeyed instructions, went out of channels to contact a former overseas handler, and said he was going to quit unless the dumb flatfeet were replaced by somebody who knew at least as much about the spy business as he did himself. There was a flap, and people got transferred around.

("Flap" is American bureaucratic slang for a panic caused by an unplanned event. I don't know its origin, but it may have to do with the image of the chickens in the barnyard flapping their wings when a hawk appears. If so, it has the same origin as "havoc," which means "hawk." Please write me if you have a better theory.)

On the other side of the Atlantic, those doubles who had been developed in the States by the FBI and were handed over to CIA for handling abroad were not used to having their personal lives supervised by a handler and were accustomed to improvise their own cases. When they found themselves reporting in detail on their day-to-day activity, there were more flaps.

But this, hurrah, is now ancient history. The law-enforcing FBI has long since learned to run doubles and to manage penetrations; CIA has learned to prepare its information in a form that will support evidence; and both have developed a system of file management and collation that makes the sharing of CI information useful to both, and to the other agencies of the U.S. government.

Nevertheless, whether you are in law enforcement or a spymaster, you will find that cops and spymasters look at the world somewhat differently. You will to some degree take on the coloration of your own organization. My advice to the cops is to assimilate some of the spymasters' qualities, and my advice to the spymasters is to get a little cop into your temperament. Then bicker and argue all you want. It will be educational for both sides. You have a lot in common, after all—you're tangling with the same enemy.

You'll also make some fine friends. Hunting, fishing, poker, chess, the opera, the theater, the PTA . . . some of my best friends are cops, and some are spymasters. I've entrusted my life to some of them, and some of them have entrusted their lives to me. We have been beaten a few times in the CI game, and we've won some, but we haven't had too many casualties. Only a few, may they rest in peace.

THE SUPPORT APPARATUS

Slang for installing a support apparatus is "putting in the plumbing." As with real plumbing, putting it in is expensive, and fixing it when something goes wrong is even more expensive. Here are some of the things that make up a counterintelligence support apparatus.

THE ROOF AND THE WALLS

Secrecy is efficiency. Secrecy is safety. Secrecy requires cover. CI people are a secretive bunch. They like to be taken for what they are not. They would much rather be taken for patent lawyers or market researchers or traffic cops than for counterspies; it makes counterspying easier. Because most of the people they are counterspying on feel the same way, CI people have a certain kinship with spies in general. If all this secrecy makes you uncomfortable, better find another line of work.

Part of cover is the apparent absence of it. Somewhere under your control should be a door with a sign, saying, in effect, "SECURITY, Enter Here and Tell All." If it is somebody else's office with which you can work closely, good. We call that kind of cover a "lightning rod," because it keeps trouble away from the door to your real office that reads, "JANITORIAL SERVICES,

Please Wipe Feet Before Entering." Journalists find this kind of evasiveness sinful, because it makes it harder for them to do their job. Our CI hearts would bleed for those hustling journalists if it were not for the fundamental difference between us: They make their living by blabbing secrets, we make ours by keeping them. General Creighton Abrams used to tell his staff that talking to journalists is like wrestling with pigs: The pigs have a lovely time, while you just get dirty.

Part of your plumbing is what the roof and walls look like that shelter you, your files, your photo lab, your offices, and the plumbing in your lavatories. I hope we have gotten away from such preposterous covers as "Center for Rehabilitation and Planning" or the U.S. Army's Counter Intelligence Corps's apocryphal "Messkit Repair Battalion."

SURVEILLANCE TEAMS

Physical surveillance, discussed in detail in chapter 7, is one of your necessary tools, whether you do it with your own staffers (as you always will do some of the time), or with specialized nonstaffers recruited, trained, and paid for the job. You have to get your surveillance facilities in place before you start working, and you have to give them continuous maintenance. Surveillance machinery, the human kind, wears out faster than flashlight batteries, and surveillance teams are not rechargeable.

THE BUG AND TAP SHOP

Technical surveillance, discussed in detail in chapter 8, is a tool of your trade and a piece of the plumbing you have to put into your CI shop. Call it the "technical section" for purposes of reporting, but what it does is service "bugs" (hidden microphones) and "taps" (gadgets that eavesdrop on signals that move through wire).

Probably the bug and tap shop will occupy an awkward amount of real estate, not only because the machines are bulky but also because maintaining them takes a big bench with a lot of sophisticated tools. It also takes at least one trained technician. If your CI unit is small, you or one of your staffers will have to be qualified for this job. In larger units, the technical section is usually separate and specialized, with people who handle all the technical equipment, including photography and disguises (see below).

SAFE HOUSES

Why not have your defectors and double agents and surveillance team chiefs come into the office (the one with the sign "JANITORIAL SERVICES")? Answer: Because you are under surveillance by the enemy—and under not so friendly observation by indigenous clerks, local policemen, transient agitators, and other people who leak almost as profusely as do the staff personnel of congressional committees in Washington. There is no sphincter control and no way to get any. Have you been to Washington lately? Noticed that pervasive smell of urine up and down the halls of the House and Senate office buildings? Now have a sniff in the corridors adjoining your office. Your French colleagues may call this experience *déjà senti*.

So you have to have safe houses and you have to have a system for establishing them and for replacing them and for maintaining them. It will be a big item in your budget and a drain on your manpower. But without them, where do you receive and handle your defectors, where do you meet your double agents, where do you coach your surveillance teams, and where do you handle the people who rent your other safe houses and hire the people who do the cleaning and laundry in them?

Some stopgaps can be used. Apartments that are temporarily vacant can be used for one-shot interrogations; colleagues working in the overt sections can be persuaded to lend their quarters one night a week while they go to the movies. But remember that whenever you improvise, security will suffer. Change safe houses often.

THE FORGERY SHOP

When I make out a check for the liquor I buy, the clerk sometimes knows me, and I don't have to show my driver's license. But most of the time the clerk has only been on the job for two weeks, doesn't know me, and is terrified of having a check bounce that she has initialed. So I have to show her "documentation" of my identity. In the spy business you have to be ready to show documentation, *false* documentation, always, wherever you are and whatever you are doing.

If you have five case officers working, each using three identities, you have eighteen identities (counting the true ones) for which you must maintain a complete set of identity documents, including the miscellaneous junk that people carry around with them. Further, you must have backup and reserve documents in additional identities for the contingencies that may arise at any moment.

For an example of how one service documented an important agent (who happened to be a corpse), see Ewen Montagu's *The Man Who Never Was* (1954, U.S. edition, 93 ff). When the agent, whose false identity was that of a William Martin, a major in the Royal Marines, was deployed from a British submarine onto the shore of neutral Spain on April 30, 1943, he carried forty-one items of documentation ranging from his two identity discs through letters from his parents and fiancee to a pencil stub. For an example of how fiction is truer than fact, read Duff Cooper's *Operation Heartbreak,* an account of the same caper.

VEHICLES

In some places where I have worked, the main vehicle for surveillance was the bicycle. But even in those places, our staffers had to have motorcars, because in those places it looked peculiar for a European or American or Japanese to move around town on a bicycle. (In the old days in Saigon, this had an advantage—the Viet Cong teams who were trained to chuck a Molotov cocktail into an obviously American sedan never could adjust to an American showing up on their turf on a bicycle. It seemed to paralyze them. How could they take seriously a capitalist bourgeois imperialist plutocrat who rode a bicycle? The man was obviously an impostor or a sympathizer.)

When you tackle the task of documenting an operational vehicle, you will be amazed at the amount of red tape, everywhere in the world, that a car is entangled with—licenses, bills of sale, insurance forms, tax receipts, repair records. You have to have a system for quick and invisible change of plates and some means of avoiding being caught with more than one set of supporting documents. How nice it is that you are ingenious and resourceful about these *absolutely essential* details. How nice that you have this bit of plumbing installed, if you do, and how dangerous if you don't.

Of course it is a little easier if you are working on your own turf—law enforcement agencies can usually manage to get blank documents for as many vehicles as they need and fill them out with whatever cover names they need; and in case of an accident, the law enforcement agency can usually arrange for the investigation to be discreet. But even these arrangements require ingenuity and attention to cover. You don't want your Traffic Violations Bureau to know your secret business before, or after, the fact.

And how nice it is overseas if you have a good working relationship with the local authorities. But be careful. You don't want them to know your secrets, either.

PHOTOGRAPHY

A photo lab is a nuisance and a bore because it has to be hidden away, yet it must have a power and water supply and must be able to function around the clock, regardless of your cover building's ostensible office hours. Another nuisance: Photo labs have a characteristic smell that tends to seep out into the corridors and into your innocent-looking receptionist's office. Exhaust fans help, if you can find a place, out of smell of the foe, to which to discharge the acetate fumes.

(Incidentally, those fumes are a problem for some agents you may be on the trail of; if they happen to do their photo work in hotel bathrooms, the smell of acetic acid can give them away, as some of us can attest who have worked on the other side of the fence.)

Can your photo lab do these chores?

- *Quick copy in volume.* A happy day in the life of a CI officer is that when a double agent or a penetration provides a sheaf of documents that have to be copied and returned in quick time. If the phototechnician who has to do the copying doesn't have the equipment and established routine to handle the job, the day is no longer a happy one.
- *Mass processing.* Surveillance teams and sometimes double agents produce a volume of negatives that must be processed instantly to be useful. Fixed photo points, which, for example, photograph everybody going in and out of a building (maybe using infrared film at night), eat up a lot of film and a lot of developing time.
- *Quick copy of small photos, for example, ID cards.* This continuing chore requires special lenses, camera stands and lights. Most shops keep a permanent set-up for this work.

- *Production of ID photos.* This continuing chore doesn't require the special equipment used in the place where you get your driver's license, but such equipment helps. Your phototechnician will pester you for it if he doesn't have it now.
- *Microdot processing.* A microdot is a tiny photonegative that can be hidden under a period on a printed or typewritten page. It normally holds an entire page of text, which has been photographed and then reduced to a size that can only be read through a microscope. Processing microdots requires specialized equipment both in your photolab and in the agent's kit. For incoming messages, the agent's own equipment can be used up to a point, but whereas the double only has to read the dot, you have to print its contents. For this you need bulky equipment. If you happen to be sending microdot instructions to a double agent or penetration, you also need relatively bulky equipment to copy your typewritten message onto a microdot negative. This is big-time stuff, and you won't lack for help from your headquarters.
- *Movie and TV.* Photosurveillance frequently uses movie techniques. When these produce movie film, your lab has to be able to develop it, project it, and make selective stills from it. When television cameras are used, projection is simpler, but making still prints requires special equipment. Still prints are essential and unavoidable. Suppose your problem is to identify your double agent's enemy handler. You have to be able to show him a selection of printed pictures ("mug book"), not hours of TV.

DROPS: LIVE, DEAD, PHONE

There are three main types of drops: live, dead, phone. Let's look at each.

Live Drops

Live drops are sometimes called "AAs," accommodation addresses, or "LBs," letter boxes. They are live because they are people, recruited agents, who receive letters or telegrams or parcels or hand-delivered material and hand it on to somebody else, whose identity is shielded behind that of the live drop. Whoever recruits and handles (pays and instructs) a live drop should himself use a false identity and if possible a false flag. Normally a live drop is recruited under a pretext—"I've got this girlfriend, see, and I can't get mail at home because of my jealous (and rich) wife. So I'll pay you a flat sum for every letter you receive for me. You'll recognize them by the funny mark at the corner of the envelope."

Remember to keep the drop alive by arranging for frequent dummy letters to be sent. This also buries the real messages among the dummies and cuts down the risk of exposure through curiosity on the part of your live drop agent, or of hope by that agent of blackmailing you, or of detection by whoever might be watching your live drop's mail for some other reason.

When you are putting in your plumbing, set up a number of live drops who will receive only dummy material until you activate them by instructing your double or penetration to use the channel. Keep a few in reserve at all times.

Finally, remember that the enemy's live drops are one of your best targets. If you can get control of an enemy live drop, you are astraddle of his communications, have your thumb on his windpipe. An enemy live drop is one of the best kinds of double agent you can have.

Dead Drops

Dead drops, sometimes called "caches," are chinks in a wall or lockers in a train station or rocks in the desert or any hiding place. The commonest items cached are rolls of microfilm and rolls of folding money, but a dead drop may contain anything from a postcard holding one microdot to a car battery in which are hidden assassination pistols, as in the Khokhlov case. (Nikolai Khokhlov was an officer in the KGB's Department of "Wet Affairs," then numbered 13, which makes a science of assassination and sabotage. The specially designed pistols that he was to use to murder an émigré leader in Germany were concealed in a car battery that was then dead-dropped for him in a locker of a Munich railway station. Fortunately for his victim, Khokhlov had an attack of conscience and defected to the victim.)

Normally when an agent has "filled" a dead drop, he gives you a signal—a chalk mark on a curbstone, a bottlecap left on a fencepost, a name underlined in a public telephone book. The whole purpose of dead drops is to avoid personal contact, which might be noticed or surveilled, between a spy and his handler. When your support agent picks up the package at the "dead-drop site," he has "serviced" the drop.

So when you are putting in the plumbing for your double agent and penetration programs, set up some dead drops, photograph them, and practice servicing them. And use your investigative resources to find your enemy's dead drops. It will not be easy—you'll need some help from your doubles.

When a double fills a dead drop for the enemy, you have two sticky problems: How can you stake it out to identify and tail whoever services it? Dare you meddle with the content of the drop? The well-trained agent preparing material to be dead-dropped booby traps it with indicators of whether it has been tampered with—a hair at a prearranged place under the scotch tape, a dusting of powder under the rim of the film cartridge. You may be dying to know what is in it—really damaging intelligence?—but you'd better not tamper. Your flaps-and-seals shop probably is not good enough to beat a KGB booby trap, as our American FBI has found out a time or two. If your surveillance team cannot cover the drop site without "blowing" (compromising) itself, let it alone.

Phone Drops

Most double agents and all penetrations lead busy lives. Their schedules cannot be made to conform with your office hours. Meeting times have to be set by the agent, not the case officer, and the efficient way to set a meeting time is by telephone. But obviously the agent cannot simply call you at your home or office; for one thing, he doesn't know either where you live or where you work, certainly not what your telephone numbers may be. And phone calls can be traced. So there must be the telephone equivalent of live and dead drops.

The simplest phone drop is a live one, an agent who takes messages and relays them to you. Sometimes the messages need be only a signal—a specified number of rings. Your phone drop agent doesn't need to answer and doesn't need to know what the signal means; he or she simply calls you a few minutes later and says that his phone sounded three rings and that this happened again three minutes later. You then know, from prearrangement with your double agent, that, for example, a meeting set for later in the evening has been canceled.

Sometimes, if you can get at the phone system at its center, you can use specialized equipment to make a kind of dead phone drop. The number given the agent may be one listed in the phone book, but your equipment cross-switches to ring somewhere else. Redialing to a long-distance number is not recommended, unless through a very good scrambler system, because most long-distance calls these days go via microwave and can be intercepted. In fact you can bet that all calls coming into your headquarters are intercepted and analyzed most skillfully by hostile services.

FLAPS AND SEALS, MICRODOT, SECRET INK

A CI service has to be able to read other people's mail without their knowledge. This means that after you have devised a way to get your hands on the mail of a suspect, you have to get it open, inspect it, maybe copy it, and get it back before he or she misses it. For this you must have expert technicians in your shop.

Spies using mail for communication often use secret writing (SW). If they are merely evading casual detection, their ink may be lemon juice or a wax paper carbon, providing just enough invisibility to fool the mail carrier or an inquisitive child. Sometimes there is no SW, as in the case of couriers signaling their itinerary by the postmark on an innocent postcard—the message is provided by the postal service.

On the other hand, the agent may use an ink devised by a nation's best chemists, one that, like a good cipher, requires a sophisticated chemical procedure to detect. If you know or suspect that sophisticated inks or microdot are in use on the mail you acquire, you probably have an important case. I shall have to leave discussion of the technology that you will use to the technicians with whom you will be working.

Flaps-and-seals work is hard on the nerves. The technician must be cautious and methodical, yet work under time pressure. This job is not unlike that of a bomb-disposal expert, and indeed (remember letter bombs?) sometimes just as dangerous.

WEAPONS

Law enforcement agencies working at home have standard procedures for the acquisition, storage, maintenance, and issue of weapons, as well as for training in their use. The CI unit working under the cover on foreign soil has problems the cop at home never dreams of.

The first rule about weapons is never carry one unless you expect—*really* expect, on the basis of solid knowledge—that you may have to use it. This applies especially to concealed handguns. A black-jack, a pair of brass knuckles, or even a fighting knife may be in a slightly different category, given the amount of street crime that goes on these days in nominally civilized places, and the amount of time your people probably have to spend on those civilized streets. You will have to make judgments day by day and hour by hour, because your people will often be carrying sensitive material that your government enjoins you to protect. Your government also expects you to protect the people themselves and to help them protect themselves.

Remember that a weapon is not much self-protection unless the bearer knows how to use it. This means not only training but also practice. A man or woman can be checked out on, say, a Browning 9-millimeter, and may at some time in the past have been able to fire it quickly and accurately. But marksmanship, like billiards, requires periodic if not constant practice, else you lose the eye, the timing, the feel of the weapon.

At home you may have a firing range in the basement of your headquarters and a regular schedule for weapons practice. Overseas, these things have to be improvised under whatever cover you have, or by ensuring that your people get weapons training and practice on their periodic trips home.

The storage and maintenance of your weapons are tasks for your support shop. Somewhere near the photo lab, the flaps-and-seals cubicle, the forgery shop, and the corner where you handle the audio equipment, there needs to be an arsenal with cleaning equipment and safe storage for ammunition.

How you get the weapons into the arsenal in the first place depends on your cover situation. Use whatever channels are available; improvise when you have to. Hope to be friendly with the local police, and be very careful if they are unfriendly.

LOCKS, KEYS, AND BURGLARY

In the early 1970s, the United States lost a whole White House full of politicians and a whole foreign policy because of a bungled burglary in a place called Watergate. The ineptitude of the retired intelligence and security people who tried to be burglars was almost as shocking as the political motive of the burglary and the criminality of the politicians who directed it.

If you, as a CI officer, are part of a law enforcement organization in your own country, you have to stay within the law—court orders, a clear chain of approving authority, and continuous judgment by yourself of the validity and necessity of each of your operations.

If you are working on foreign soil, your operations are by definition illegal under the laws of your host country, no matter how many agreements have been signed between your service and the host government. In either case, you must have the resources available to commit what is euphemisticly called "surreptitious entry."

The ultimate objective of burglary in the CI business is to steal information, either directly by filching or copying documents, or by installing surveillance devices (see chapter 8) that will steal information for you. You will therefore use the people who can be integrated into a particular caper—surveillants, photo technicians, flappers and sealers, forgers and disguisers (to give your burglars some cover), and so on. But you must also have people trained in penetrating physical security barriers, whether simple locks that can be picked with a piece of coat hanger wire or the electronic sensing systems that normally surround a communications room. And these people must be backed up by a good workshop stocked with the tools of the locksmith's trade. It does no harm for every one of your case officers, and you, to have some basic training in locks and picks—know how to use a "rake," understand the principle of the pin-barrel lock and the master system keys that can be made from a single example borrowed from an accessible door in a target building, know how safe combinations are set and how a safe lock works, and understand the rudiments of the electronic sensing that insulates some meeting rooms against audio surveillance.

DISGUISES

The rebirth of the fashion for face hair (after—was it the Korean War?) was a boon for people who have to evade surveillance, and a calamity for surveillants. Regiments of spies who had been wearing mustaches and even some with beards immediately shaved themselves clean so that they could change the shape of their faces with false hair as the moment required. Brown beards in the morning turned blond at noon and red in the evening. Mustaches altered hourly from toothbrush to handlebar to guardsman.

Childish? Melodramatic? Well, even outside a Victorian thriller, disguise has its place. The hidden movie camera that films you leaving your building can often be confused by a change of clothing, a beard of a different color, or a limp from a marble in your shoe. So can the foot team tailing you.

Smuggling a defector from an official building to a waiting automobile is easier if you change his appearance. Both he and you are less likely to have a fatal collision with a truck or catch a round from a sniper.

So, somewhere in your shop near the flaps-and-seals bench you may need a cosmetic stand equipped with wigs and hair dye and false beards. There must also be a wardrobe of varied clothing, and each of your case officers (and your surveillance team) should keep an assortment of the kind of clothes worn by the local population, not neglecting that giveaway, shoes. A *Steireranzug* (gray and green costume) common in Austria is not much good on the streets of Vienna if the shoes are made by Florsheim. Austrians always look at shoes, and they know what non-Austrian shoes look like.

5

INTERROGATION: HOW IT
REALLY WORKS

THE MYTH OF TORTURE

Movies about World War II show sadistic Gestapo men gouging out the eyes of the heroic civilians of the French Resistance. Movies about revolutions in Latin America show men and women beaten until they faint from pain, are revived with buckets of bloody water, dragged back to their cells, then dragged to the interrogation chamber and beaten again. In fact movies dramatizing torture are so popular that one wonders who the real sadists are, the characters or the audience.

But those movies, whatever their moral or propaganda intent may be, are hogwash as far as real interrogation is concerned. Take it from an old hand at interrogation (starting in World War II), those Gestapo torturers, many of whom really existed, never got more than a pfennig's worth of information from their prisoners. Ditto today's sinister stumblebums in country X (you name it), many of whom also exist.

Why doesn't torture work? Because a person in pain is not an accurate reporter. Ask any doctor.

In the Middle Ages the purpose of torture was not to acquire information. It was to punish criminals, political enemies, or heretics; to get revenge; to demonstrate power; and to have fun. Confessions were obtained, as they are today, to whatever crimes the interrogators already knew about or found it useful to invent. The purpose of torture, where used today in the name of interrogation, is the same. Torture does not produce information, much less control of a potential agent or double agent.

Make no mistake, interrogation of any kind is a dirty business. It degrades, debases, and humiliates the person being interrogated, because it intrudes on his or her privacy. And that means that it also degrades and debases (and should humiliate, i.e., make humble) the interrogator.

Interrogation is such a dirty business that it should be done only by people of the cleanest character. If you have any sadistic tendencies yourself, please get out of the business now. Read no further. Go pull the wings off butterflies, or something, far away from counterintelligence. We don't want you for a colleague.

THE COMPLEAT INTERROGATOR

Here are some of the talents and traits of character that a good interrogator must have:

- General knowledge of all the other disciplines of CI
- Experience in analysis of file material
- A working knowledge of psychology
- Understanding of himself and control of his own emotions
- Some acting ability, with an actor's sense of timing
- Patience

The person who enjoys hurting is a lousy interrogator in even the most human situation. But the humane person who shrinks from *manipulating* his or her subject is also a lousy interrogator.

Think of interrogation as a kind of judo. Judo works on the principle that you turn your opponent's strength against her. She charges at you, and you use her momentum to flip her on her ear. But you have to know what her strengths are, or you can't do it. And you have to know how to make her charge.

The interrogator, like a priest or a doctor, must have a talent for empathy, a personal need to communicate with other people, a concern for what makes other people tick even when he is putting maximum emotional pressure on them. His anger, his indignation, his disgust toward his prisoner must always be tempered by the kind of attitude a doctor has toward a patient; he may hate that patient, but he knows how the patient got to be hateful, and he keeps his own hatred off to one side.

Conversely, if he finds the prisoner likeable, he must put his friendly feeling aside. Especially if the prisoner happens to be of the opposite gender and winsome. The number of interrogators who have been bamboozled since the dawn of history by the body language and appealing manner of pretty prisoners is, to be precise, 43,123,465; in the time it has taken to write this sentence, that number has increased by 314.

Incidentally, though we seem to be assuming here that all interrogators are men, the same rules apply to women. Women interrogators are a minority, but those who get into the trade are usually very good, probably because they often have a background in case analysis and detection in which no nonsense is permitted yet have the talent for establishing rapport that men call feminine intuition.

PRESSURE

We said that physical pain is not relevant in interrogation. Anxiety, humiliation, loneliness, and pride are another story.

When the Chinese in Korea, and the North Vietnamese a few years later, wanted to brainwash a prisoner, they did not use pain. They used discomfort, hunger, and humiliation, combined with one of the worst tortures of all: solitude. When, after a few weeks alone in a cramped cell, you are hungry and have no toilet paper, no toothbrush, no way to fight the lice and fleas, no sense of how much time has passed, no blanket against the night chill, and *nobody to talk to,* you are putty in the hands of the first person who says "Good morning. How are you feeling? I need your help."

Not you, you say? Try it some time. You will acquire knowledge about that basic trick of the CI officer's trade called interrogation. This is knowledge that a CI officer must have to do her job. Why? There are two reasons: She has to prepare people (and herself) to withstand interrogation, and she has to use her knowledge in effectively doing her own interrogations.

Not all interrogations are in prisons, you say? Wrong. *Psychologically,* all persons being interrogated are prisoners, or else it is not an interrogation but an interview or a debriefing.

Your first job, and one that continues throughout every case, is to get on top of all pertinent investigative material and, as the case progresses, to review it continually along with the information and misinformation you are getting by interrogation. Your files should be your main weapon against your subject. With them you know what you know, and your subject does not know what you know. As interrogation proceeds and the patterns get complicated, the subject usually forgets what he has said and often begins to contradict himself. This process of confusion can be helped along by the interrogator's planting false ideas of what is in his files.

During the Cold War, the Soviet-dominated intelligence services sometimes mechanized this process by forcing their prisoners to write statements again and again, which were then compared for discrepancies that were used in interrogation as pressure devices.

Your second job is to arrange things so that your subject feels he is a prisoner. The husband in the cartoon coming home from a night on the town is, psychologically, the prisoner of his irate wife. He has no place to go and he has to answer up. If he walks out or tells her to go to hell or gives her a good thrashing, she has failed as an interrogator, at least momentarily. The next morning may find him back at the doorstep (back in prison) and repentant, in which case she is on the way to succeeding.

This means you must interrogate on your own turf. If you have to work on your subject's turf, take charge of it. Put a guard on the door; have an assistant come in and out with a visible notebook or tape recorder; move the furniture around so that you have the most comfortable chair; give yourself room to walk around, but keep the subject sitting.

You'll think of other tricks to fit your immediate situation. Use them to make your subject feel isolated, cut off from his or her normal environment, alone with only you to talk to. Remember that every *normal* person is conditioned from childhood to want to converse. That need to talk and have somebody respond, and to respond to somebody else is built into what we call human nature.

Your third job in an interrogation is to make your prisoner act on his or her urge to talk to you, if only to lie. Remember, you are being paid to be lied to. So your problem is to figure out what makes your subject tick. Examples:

- *Pride:* Is she proud of her work? Then get her to correct *your* misconceptions about it. Let her teach you, lecture you, sneer at you for your ignorance, but keep her talking.
- *Shame:* Is he ashamed of something he has done? Then show him gently how he can expiate his shame without losing your respect. Let him indulge his shame and his self-pity, but keep him talking.
- *Fear #1:* Is she frightened of reprisals from colleagues? Then get her to help you plan how

to protect her. (Do *not* brag that *your* service
can always protect her; it probably isn't true, and
anyway you may need her anxiety later as a tool
against her.) When she has become your partner
in planning her own protection (and conspiring
against her former friends), she will feel obligated
to be your partner in everything else.

• *Fear #2:* Is he afraid of you and what you may do
to him? Then get him to help you with your job;
explain that you do not want to punish him, you
only want information, and he must help you avoid
having to punish him. Threats must be implied,
not stated. Explain that you must, reluctantly,
enforce the "rules of the game."

THE SCHMIDT STORY

Here is a story to illustrate, among other things, a relatively
humane use of emotionally stressful interrogation. There was a
dishonest Abwehr (Nazi German intelligence) officer in World
War II who made a modest career from getting the London
and New York newspapers at a post in Western Europe (which
I am forbidden to name) before they arrived in Berlin. Having this advance information (I'll call him Schmidt), Schmidt
invented a net of agents that allegedly collected information
about the shipment of ammunition and sensitive supplies
across the Atlantic and concocted a series of reports to his
Abwehr superiors in Berlin. When the newspapers arrived in
Berlin a few days later, fragments of information in them appeared to corroborate Schmidt's reports, and so he was repeatedly promoted.

But the war ended, and Schmidt was out of a job. Also out
of a job was a colleague of his ("Müller"), who had sat at a desk
at Abwehr headquarters in Berlin throughout the war and who

knew all that the Germans knew, as of the end of the war, about the Soviet Air Force. So Schmidt and Müller teamed up to get themselves on the payroll of an Allied intelligence service. They set up an office in Germany, subscribed to all the Allied magazines on air technology (of which there were, and are, an astonishingly indiscreet number), invented a network of secret agents in the Soviet Union, and began producing reports on all the latest designs for Soviet aircraft.

At first Schmidt's reports were enthusiastically received by Allied intelligence, but as time went by, they seemed to be less and less consistent with reports from other sources. Schmidt came under suspicion, and an Allied CI officer was called in to investigate him.

The first job, as always, was file research. At a library of captured German documents that had been assembled by Allied services, the CI officer (or the analyst working with him) found a record of an investigation of Schmidt conducted in 1944 by the Abwehr, which had become suspicious when none of the ships carrying bombs and bomber engines that Schmidt had reported had been located by German submarines. Oddly, the German investigation had been called off when Schmidt's friend Müller had interceded. The CI officer then checked on Müller and found him living in a West German city with an office to which frequent packages of French, American, and British magazines were delivered.

Interrogation was now in order. Using the extraordinary police powers of the occupation forces, the Allied CI officer caused Schmidt to be secretly arrested, blindfolded, driven aimlessly around for an hour, and then confined, alone, in the empty and windowless wine cellar of a castle. His bed was one blanket on the stone floor (it was summer, but nights in the wine cellar were chilly). His latrine was a large tin can. He had no razor, no toothbrush, no mirror. His light, which burned continuously, was one bulb hanging from the ceiling. His food was fed to him irregularly, though plentifully, through a slot in the door, and his guards were forbidden to speak to him. And so he sat, on the floor, for a number of days.

One afternoon, or morning, or night—Schmidt had lost track of time—a guard came into the wine cellar and covered Schmidt's head with a pillowcase, tying it around his waist. The Allied CI officer (who spoke accentless German), then entered and, invisible, began the interrogation: "Glad to see you in such good health. Do you have any questions?"

"Where am I?"

"You'll never know."

"What happens next?"

"Depends on you."

"What do you want from me?"

"You know what I want."

"I need a toothbrush."

"Sorry. Have to go now. I'll be back."

"When?"

"You'll know when I come back."

More days and nights went by. When the CI officer came back, he brought a typewriter and a ream of paper.

"I'm leaving a typewriter and some paper. You'll find it when they take off the pillowcase. Write me what I want to know."

"What's that?"

"Call it 'The Schmidt Story.'"

When he came back, the CI officer found a couple of dozen typed pages beside the typewriter. He tore them up without reading and left.

How long did this game go on? Weeks? Months? Eventually, the Schmidt story reached three hundred pages—all factual, all fascinating—and it also included the Müller story, which Müller had also typed up in a similar cellar in a different castle with a different pillowcase, but the same interrogator, who had expended about three hours a week on the whole operation.

Separately, Schmidt and Müller were blindfolded, driven around for an hour in their separate cities, and set free with some pocket money to get started afresh. Neither ever again went into the business of fabricating intelligence.

Was torture used? Well, Schmidt and Müller had an uncomfortable time of it, and they lost a lot of self-esteem. But they were resilient men. When his conscience ached a little, the CI officer told himself that he would never have used that method on anybody who had not already proven himself a tough and agile survivor. Many years later in a different part of the world, the interrogator became a casual friend of Schmidt, though Schmidt never knew that his latter-day friend was his erstwhile enemy.

WHEN THE TRICKS DON'T WORK

There are three kinds of people against whom the foregoing tricks do not always work: sociopaths, veterans of torture, and professional intelligence officers. Here are some tips.

Sociopaths

The category of sociopaths includes pathological liars and habitual criminals. They may be quite bright and quite well informed, but they are ruled by a need to dominate their immediate surroundings from moment to moment in disregard of the consequences of their behavior. Their weakness is that when they lose control of the person-to-person situation, they will go to great lengths (even telling the truth) to get back their feeling of control. What often upsets them and starts them on the road to cooperating is for the interrogator to shrug his or her shoulders, say that the prisoner is too trivial to waste time on, and pretend to end the interrogation. Sociopaths suffer when they are dismissed with bored contempt. They then seek to enlist their interrogator in some kind of conspiracy that they can dominate. Playing their game with them from this point on is tricky, but necessary.

Veterans of Torture

A survivor of prolonged brutal interrogation at the hands, say, of the Gestapo in France, the Japanese in Malaya, or the KGB in the Lubianka has probably survived because he learned a trick of self-hypnosis, an ability to go limp, to turn off the mind. Whatever you call it ("voluntary autism"?), it stops an interrogation dead.

When are you likely to encounter such veterans of torture? More often than you might think. Examples: (1) a Central American peasant who has been brutalized by a police interrogation that provided him with a motive to join a communist guerilla group, from which he was recruited and trained as a General Directorate of Intelligence (Cuban Intelligence Service) agent to work in, say, Puerto Rico; (2) a Slovak Jewish survivor of Auschwitz recruited by the Czech Intelligence Service to serve as an agent in Israel.

With such prisoners, however, you have the advantage of *not* being in the torture business; and, with patience, the contrast between your interrogation and the old brutal ones can be brought home to the prisoner. Here is the point at which you should abandon threats altogether. If you can't get cooperation using friendship, realism, and analysis, give up. But if you work at it properly, you will probably find that you don't have to give up. Genuine humane sympathy for someone who has been tortured is easy to feel and easy to convey, and it makes for a powerful bond between interrogator and prisoner.

Professional Intelligence Officers

No subject is more difficult or more fun to interrogate than a pro from a hostile service. He knows your tricks, he knows the material, he knows what he can throw away and what he must protect, and he has so much information that he can easily deflect you from the more important to the trivial, or from the generally true to the specifically false. Assume from the beginning that *a pro may bend but will never break* (see "The Breaking Point" below.) Even the true defector will have some secrets that for private reasons—shame, loyalty to old comrades, plans for his own use of the information—he will never give you, and sometimes those secrets are important ones. Even Schmidt, whose story is told above, kept some secrets that we learned only much later, including the important one that Müller had a wartime connection with Soviet intelligence through the Schulze-Boysen group in Berlin. (Oberleutnant Harro Schulze-Boysen was a Soviet penetration of the headquarters of German Air Force Intelligence until his detection and execution in 1942).

"Legal" intelligence officers—those with diplomatic immunity—have "legends" (cover stories) built into their "cover," like second secretary, cultural officer, and the like. And they will often have a "throwaway" legend by which they admit to being less important spies than they really are.

"Illegals," on the other hand, usually depend on being inconspicuous to avoid detection and have trouble supporting their cover once caught. With some good detective work and analysis, their documents can usually be shown to be false, and their ostensible means of earning a living can be exposed as improbable.

Kolon Molodiy, a KGB illegal who worked in London as "Gordon Arnold Lonsdale," the proprietor of a business that sold pinball machines, was documented with the identity of a dead Canadian. When the birth records were checked in Canada, it was found that the real Gordon Lansdale had been circumcised, whereas London's "Gordon Lonsdale" had his foreskin intact. This bit of detective work by the Mounties was welcomed by Molodiy's interrogators in London. But Molodiy clammed up and the interrogators got little information from him to expand their case against his illegal *rezidentura*.

Interrogation of professional intelligence officers like Molodiy is tough, but in one respect the job is easy, because early rapport with a pro is almost automatic. An oil geologist from Texas talks the same basic language as a rival from Iran. They may be at swords' points, but they understand each other. So it is with pros in the spy business. After the first few minutes, interrogating a pro is a combination of chess and judo. Good luck.

THE BREAKING POINT

Interrogators talk about "breaking" a subject. This is shorthand for inducing a subject to decide to tell all, to stop lying and evading, to take his medicine, to submit to your direction. The breaking is often traumatic, with symptoms of a nervous breakdown.

When a subject "breaks," the interrogation is over, theoretically. From here on out, theoretically, you are debriefing him or training him to be double agent or recording his confession for use in his trial. But in reality, an interrogation never ends. When an interrogator and a sometime subject meet, months or years later, invisible prison walls spring up around them.

And so it should be, if the interrogator has done his or her job. Mind you, there may be handclasps and embraces and goodwill all around, but those prison walls are still there. And if the subject's job is now that of double agent, the interrogator had better remember that his or her own job is now that of case officer. The old job of interrogation is now one of agent testing and agent handling and protection of an agent's life. Interrogation has become counterespionage.

HOW TO MANAGE THE POLYGRAPH

People in the news media, who do not like to admit that they make their living in a branch of the entertainment industry—which is funded by the advertising industry—do a lot of heavy breathing about the polygraph machine, which they usually call the "lie detector." And the news media are the sea in which politicians swim, so politicians also huff strong and puff hard about the "lie detector," on which they seldom bother to inform themselves. The fashionable attitude is sanctimonious indignation.

A staunchly patriotic secretary of state can say, "The minute in this government that I am told that I am not trusted is the day that I leave.... I have grave reservations about the so-called lie detector test. It is hardly a scientific instrument. It tends to identify people who are innocent as guilty and misses some fraction of people who are guilty of lying. It is, I think, pretty well demonstrated that a professional spy or professional leaker can probably train himself or herself not to be caught by the test" (George Shultz, December 19, 1985, quoted by the Associated Press). I propose here to talk not about the ethics of the polygraph as an interrogation tool but about the realities of its use.

WHAT THE POLYGRAPH IS

The polygraph is a measuring instrument, nothing more. It combines three (hence "poly," meaning "many") medical devices, which measure (1) blood pressure and pulse, (2) rate of perspiration, and (3) breathing pattern. Each device is connected to a mechanical writing pen loaded with red ink, called a stylus, and the three pens trace lines simultaneously on a chart that is scrolled across a viewer. It is thus similar to many instruments that medics use to diagnose your brain waves (electroencephalograph), your heart performance (electrocardiograph), and the like. (Indeed, these instruments may be incorporated in a future, more sophisticated polygraph instrument.) The whole machine, with extra paper, ink, plug adapters, and a tool kit, makes a package about like that of what used to be called a "portable" computer. Among polygraph operators in the field, the incidence of hernias is high, as they lug their "portable" machines from office to car and from safe house to safe house.

The *blood pressure* component is the commonplace rubber bladder that the doc wrapped around your upper arm the last time you had a physical examination. He pumped it full of air to choke your circulation a little so that the resultant air pressure would register on a dial. The polygraph simply uses a stylus instead of a dial. Changes of blood pressure are scratched by the stylus on the moving chart, and the *pulse rate* is automatically shown, because the blood pressure rises and then drops off a little (systole/diastole) with each pumping of the heart.

Measurement of *perspiration* depends on the fact that your sweat contains salt, and salt is a conductor of electricity. The more sweat the more salt, and if you run an electric current through it, the more sweat the more electricity, which is measurable by a galvanometer or ammeter affixed to the palm of your hand, which in turn translates your changes of sweat rate into the movement of the second stylus writing on the chart.

Breathing has two aspects, frequency and depth. The pattern of these two is registered by the third stylus from a flexible belt that is fastened, with mild discomfort, around your chest. If you hold your breath, the chart shows it. If you breathe more shallowly, the chart records it. If you take a deep breath, as most of us do every minute or so (and as we do when we feel a sense of relief), the chart shows it.

The chart shows how these three reactions occur in relation to each other. Your blood pressure and your perspiration may increase at the same time, or they may not, and you may or may not breathe more shallowly at the same time.

The fourth factor, which relates to these three, is the *verbal stimulus* injected by the interrogator, which he or she notes on the chart with a felt-tip pen while speaking it.

HOW THE POLYGRAPH WORKS

If you are riding as passenger in a car when a child suddenly darts in front of you, your blood pressure will rise, you will perspire through the palms of your hands, and you will hold your breath while the driver brakes or swerves. If you could be hooked up to a polygraph during this experience and the moving chart with its three pens could be shown on a split screen beside the view through the windshield, the blood pressure and sweat lines would make sharp peaks, and the breathing line would jump suddenly (as you "catch your breath"), then drop to a trough. There would be a lag between your seeing the child and changes on the chart that could be measured and studied, as your reaction time, by a physician interested in your reflexes. If you had been drinking heavily or had drugs in your system, the physician (or an experienced polygraph operator) could detect the alcohol or narcotics by studying that lag of reaction time.

All this only restates what you already know—that what you see and hear affects the way your heart and skin and lungs work from moment to moment. You can compare it with the quick leap of the deer in my backyard when they see my neighbor's dog or hear him bark. But there is a difference between you and the deer, because a lot of what you see (reading this page, for example) and a lot of what you hear are *words*. And words, or the meaning in them, also affect your body's functioning.

Let us hook you up to a polygraph machine and read you a list of words: "wood . . . glass . . . water . . . God . . . cloud . . . lightbulb . . . sex . . . paper . . . shoe."

Now look at the chart, on which the operator has scribbled each word as he spoke it. Will there be mountains and valleys? Unless you are an unusual person, there will be two little mountains of blood and two little mountains of sweat, each named "God" and "Sex," and two little valleys of breathing with the same names; and after the list is completed, there will be a mountain made by the third stylus showing your sigh of relief that the reading of the list is over.

Now suppose that instead of reading you a list of names, we asked you a series of short questions to which you are required to answer "Yes" or "No" (in this case we have *not* rehearsed the questions with you beforehand):

1. "Is it raining?"
2. "Are you wearing shoes?"
3. "Was Abraham Lincoln a president?"
4. "Do you like this polygraph machine?"
5. "Do you speak English?"
6. "Do you smoke?"
7. "Are you wearing clothing?"
8. "Are you a Russian spy?"
9. "Is baseball a game?"

To each of these questions, except number 8, let us say you have answered "Yes." As he or she asked each question, the operator has scribbled its number on the moving chart, and now looks at the mountains and valleys. He or she finds nothing special on 1, 2, and 3; a moderate reaction on 4; nothing much on 5; a slight reaction on 6; nothing on 7 and 9—but a big reaction on 8.

WHY DO YOU REACT TO THE POLYGRAPH?

Some psychologists theorize that your blood pressure rises higher when hearing "God" than when hearing "light bulb" because the *concept* of "God," whatever it is in your mind, has emotional and intellectual connotations greater than those of "lightbulb." Your reaction to "God" therefore uses more circuits in your computer-like brain, burning more chemical energy there, *and also in your body,* because brain and body are connected through the vagus nerve and your glandular system (e.g., the adrenal gland).

A medical researcher in Boston (Dr. Andrew P. Selwyn, of Brigham and Women's Hospital) has demonstrated that mental arousal of any kind—doing arithmetic in your head, for example—often causes "ischemia," a painless contraction of the heart's arteries that damages the heart muscle and contributes to eventual heart failure in some patients. Heart damage from undergoing a polygraph interrogation is therefore a risk, about the same as your reciting the multiplication tables or my thinking through the writing of this sentence.

The same psychologists believe that, *in most people, not all,* the brain must use more electrochemical energy to answer a question falsely than to tell the truth. It simply has to consult more of its libraries and use more of its circuits while formulating a response.

Other psychologists lay more emphasis on *guilt conditioning,* a newfangled term for "conscience." They say that your reaction to the word "sex" is stronger than to "shoes" because you have been conditioned since birth to think of sex in ethical and moral terms, and to feel guilty about your own sexual behavior.

The polygraph operator working overseas learns to modify this theory somewhat. He or she finds that it applies uniformly to the sexual consciousness of northern Europeans, natives of the British Isles, and Americans, who share a common "guilt culture," but less so to Latin Americans, southern Europeans, and Middle Eastern Muslims, and that it applies hardly at all to Southeast Asian non-Christians.

Fortunately, however, sex is not everything. In most (not all) cultures, speaking the truth is a virtue and lying is a vice. Even with those subjects whose culture has conditioned them to say, out of politeness, what will please their host, whether true or false, the experienced operator can create an interpersonal situation in which the subject feels obligated to speak truth to the interrogator—whether polite or not.

With some ethnically alien individuals (Javanese mystics come to mind), the basic difference between what we Westerners think of as truth and falsehood is simply not there. For them the polygraph will not work as a lie detector. Nevertheless, the polygraph can be used on them as a tool for psychological assessment and can thereby support the other investigative tools, as we shall discuss later in this book.

Note our use of terms like "culture" and "ethnically alien." This shows that when working outside his or her own country, or with subjects with backgrounds different from his or hers, a counterintelligence officer has to know what makes a subject tick, and so has to know where they are coming from. A CI officer cannot be a missionary, and had better not try, but has to be an anthropologist.

WHAT YOUR REACTIONS MEAN

We are assuming, for purposes of demonstration, that your case is a simple one, and that you are an American or North European or Briton, are sober and clean of drugs, and that a psychiatrist would think you are mentally healthy. What is the operator's conclusion from your chart?

You answered question number 8 to the effect that you are *not* a Russian spy. But your blood pressure went up, your palms sweated, and you held your breath as you answered it.

Well, the operator's conclusion is *not* that you were lying and that you really are a Russian spy. If he knows his trade, he concludes only that the idea of being a Russian spy upsets you, maybe because you really are one, or maybe because you just hate Russian spies or hate the degrading idea of being one. He puts your reaction in the same category as your weaker reaction to question number 6. On 6, he knows your answer is truthful, that you do smoke, but he also knows that these days all smokers are made to feel defensive about smoking, and when you say, in effect, "Yes, I smoke," you have a conditioned twinge of defensive anger about it.

In the case of question number 4, you have lied in saying that you like this machine you are strapped into. Nobody likes to take a polygraph test, and trying to be polite to the operator will not change your emotional reaction to it. But even if you had decided not to be polite and to say "No!" your chart would probably still have scratched blood-sweat mountains and a breathing valley after that question simply because you feel so strongly about the uncomfortable and ego-degrading machine that you are strapped into.

As a lie detector, then, in this test using nine *surprise* questions, the polygraph would have failed. As a means of learning something about your personality, on the other hand, it would have been useful.

But suppose that the nine questions have been discussed with you before the test begins, and you have put on record the answer you will give to each one. Your mental state is now different, because you have already recorded your answers and know that you are now being held responsible for their accuracy. If you know, or believe, that your answers are accurate, the emotional strain of answering will be less. Your brain, and the body wired into it, will use less energy.

Note what the "pre-exam" discussion has done for your peace of mind. Guilt feelings about smoking (question number 6) have been discussed and put into perspective. You have agreed to answer "No" to question number 4, because you really hate the polygraph machine. The meaning of being a "Russian spy" has been defined to eliminate all vague feelings of friendship toward the USSR or intellectual judgments about communism and to specify conspiratorial activity using the tradecraft of espionage—secret meetings, secret communications, theft of information, spotting other agent candidates, and so on. In fact, because "Russian spy" are dirty words to most people (except professional Soviet intelligence officers), you have agreed with the operator to rephrase question number 8 in more precise, less emotionally charged language: "Are you a controlled agent of the Soviet Intelligence Service?"

What does your chart look like—now quite different from the one you would have made if the questions had all been surprises? Here are the questions and your answers:

1. "Is it raining?" *Yes*
2. "Are you wearing shoes?" *Yes*
3. "Was Abraham Lincoln a president?" *Yes*
4. "Do you like this polygraph machine?" *No*
5. "Do you speak English?" *Yes*
6. "Do you smoke?" *Yes*
7. "Are you wearing clothing?" *Yes*
8. "Are you a controlled agent of the Soviet Intelligence Service? *No*
9. "Is baseball a game?" *Yes*

Your chart looks like table 6.1.

Table 6.1 Results of a Lie Detector Test Using Nine Surprise Questions

Question	Blood Pressure	Pulse Rate	Perspiration	Breathing
			Effect on	
1.	Slight rise	Slight rise	Slight increase	Slight decline
	(Interpretation: Normal nervousness at beginning of test.)			
2.	Return to norm	Return to norm	Return to norm	Return to norm
	(Interpretation: No stress. Relief.)			
3.	No change	No change	No change No change	
	(Interpretation: No stress.)			
4.	Slight rise	Slight rise	Slight increase	Slight decline
	(Interpretation: Slight resentment of the machine as ego threat.)			
5.	Return to norm	Return to norm	Return to norm	Return to norm
	(Interpretation: No stress. Relief.)			
6.	Slight rise	Slight rise	Slight increase	Slight decline
	(Interpretation: Slight guilt feeling about smoking.)			
7.	Return to norm	Return to norm	Return to norm	Return to norm
	(Interpretation: No stress. Relief.)			
8.	Moderate rise	Moderate rise	Moderate increase	Moderate decline
	(Interpretation: Distaste for the idea in the question?) Untruthful answer would produce stronger reaction?)			
9.	Return to norm	Return to norm	Return to norm	Deep breath
	(Interpretation: No stress. Relief at end of test.)			

KNOWN LIES AND SURPRISE QUESTIONS

In the example of nine questions used above, your operator may feel uncertain about that critical question number 8. He has noticed a "moderate" reaction, which he thinks is probably just "distaste for the idea in the question," because, maybe, "an untruthful answer would produce a stronger reaction?" But what about that question mark? How can he be sure that the reaction, in this particular subject, is not actually a strong one?

To be sure of his own judgment, he needs to know what a really strong reaction looks like in his particular subject, you. One way is to see your reactions to a *known lie,* one in which he knows you are lying and knows that you do not know that he knows. Fortunately for him, and also for you, he has material provided by the investigator in charge of your case. He knows one of your private secrets, unimportant to him, but important to you. To qualify for a loan on a house, you once falsified your financial statement to the bank, claiming to own a block of stock that actually belonged to your mother. No matter that you never defaulted on the loan, that the bank's loan officer had encouraged you to make the false statement, that you later inherited the stock—it was a false statement and you know it was a false statement and you have always been ashamed and afraid to reveal your falsehood, even to your spouse. Furthermore, you do not know that a routine investigation of your background has turned up the falsehood. The polygraph operator, coached by the investigator managing the interrogation, can gamble that you will lie about it.

The operator therefore tells you that he would like to run another set of questions, and he proposes a set much like the first, except that question number 8 now reads, "Have you ever falsified a financial statement to a bank?" He hopes that your answer will be the false one, "No," and is pleased when you indicate that "No" will be your answer.

Without telling you, the operator also decides to use a surprise question at the end of the series. From the test he has just run (question number 4), he knows that you hate, and therefore probably fear, the machine itself. When he has finished the agreed-on series of questions, he therefore keeps the machine running and says that he has one more question. He pauses and watches while your blood pressure rises, your sweating increases, and your breathing becomes shallow in anticipation of some question that you vaguely imagine—"Have you ever masturbated? Did you lie to your mother? Have you lied to me . . . ?"—and when the red lines on the chart seem to have reached maximum of peaks and troughs, he asks, "Have you brushed your teeth?"

What a dirty trick! I *said* that interrogation is a dirty business. Note how completely you, the voluntary subject, have been a *prisoner* throughout this procedure.

What the chart now shows is a couple of maximum responses—one from a known lie, the other from fear. They can be compared with your answer to the previous question numbers. If they are stronger than your answer to the question about whether you are a Soviet agent, the investigator managing the case can add this bit of information to all the rest that points to the likelihood that you are a normal, loyal citizen. Thank you, Mr. Secretary; your colleagues appreciate your support.

From the above, you will have concluded that a polygraph operator needs to be a person of unusual experience and knowledge that go beyond just knowing how to push the buttons and twist the knobs. You may also have decided that some polygraph operators are probably more skillful than others. You are right.

Every polygraph operator should believe in his or her heart that he or she and her or his machine are fallible, that they make mistakes, that no operator can possibly know enough medicine, psychology, electronics, CI, anthropology, and geography to be infallible. To managers of polygraph interrogations my advice is: If your operator believes that he is running a perfect lie detector, fire him. He doesn't know his business.

On the other hand, if he thinks of his machine and of his skills as a way of *assisting investigation, of providing leads,* use him, work with him, help him.

WHEN THE POLYGRAPH WORKS AS A LIE DETECTOR

The favorite example cited in training courses of a polygraph working as a true lie detector is that of a suspect in a murder. The operator knows that the weapon was a knife, but this has been kept secret by the police. Here are the questions and answers:

1. Are you wearing clothes? *Yes*
2. Did you commit the murder? *No*
3. Did you use a club? *No*
4. Did you use a gun? *No*
5. Did you use a knife? *No*
6. Did you use poison? *No*
7. Did you use your hands? *No*
8. Are you wearing shoes? *Yes*

Because only the murderer and the police know that question number 5 is the critical one, the suspect's chart (if he is a normal person, not drunk, not under narcotics) will conclusively show whether he is guilty. He either "kicks" on number 5 or he doesn't. If he is the murderer, it doesn't matter whether he feels guilty about the crime—he remembers that knife and he knows it may have gotten him into bad trouble.

Would that all polygraph tests were that simple, especially in CI work, where your subjects are usually complicated human beings in complicated situations, often in an alien environment.

In my own experience, off and on for twenty-six years managing (and taking) polygraph examinations, I have only known one case in which the machine functioned as a perfect lie detector, and that was on a person with a most peculiar physical makeup. She was a middle-aged, rather mousy north European Protestant woman living under a false name with false documents in Western Europe whom we had identified through routine research and surveillance as the operator of an agent radio link for an Eastern European intelligence service. Because we already knew her status as a spy, the purpose of the polygraph test was to force her to confess it so that we could debrief her and recruit her as a double agent against her parent service. (See chapter 10 on recruiting double agents.) To my astonishment, and that of the operator, her heart stopped beating for two full beats when she gave a false answer to the first critical question, "Is your name . . .?" And her heart skipped two beats on every false answer thereafter. When the questions were over, the operator simply tore the chart out of the machine, pointed to the level place opposite his first question, and said, "Now what the hell *is* your name?" She told him, and in time she became a valuable double agent (see chapter 11).

This was one case in a million, maybe 10 million. Don't count on ever getting one like it.

WHEN THE POLYGRAPH DOES NOT WORK

In chapter 5, in discussing interrogation, we noted three kinds of subjects on whom standard interrogation tricks are of little use: sociopaths, professional intelligence officers, and veterans of torture. With these, the polygraph can be very useful—not as a lie detector, but as a support to investigation.

Sociopaths

In a sense, all statements by sociopaths are lies. A bizarre pattern of answers to polygraph questions (which you will also get from a schizophrenic on the verge of or in the throes of an episode) will instantly expose the sick condition. The trick is to identify not what is true but what the subject wants to be true. As CI information, this is quite as useful for analysis as that from a normal subject.

Professional Intelligence Officers

A professional trained to use self-hypnosis or biofeedback to neutralize the polygraph can usually be recognized at the outset from the very flatness of his or her reactions. Further, these yoga tricks don't work against properly prepared surprise questions. When you find your subject using autosuggestion, you have already learned enough about him or her to restructure your investigation.

Veterans of Torture

If the subject, who has learned to go limp under forceful interrogation, can be persuaded to take a polygraph test, he will react quite normally, for a polygraph test is an interactive procedure, and if the subject gives up his limpness, he has surrendered to the machine.

Emotionally Fatigued Subjects

Your operator will urge you to keep the interrogations short because he or she knows that a subject can only react to questions for a limited time. "He'll run out of adrenalin," the operator will say. So use the polygraph sparingly, and only when you have prepared your questions carefully.

CAN YOU BEAT THE POLYGRAPH?

Tranquillizers, barbiturates, alcohol, and various other narcotics can be used to bollix up the body's reactions to polygraph questions, but the experienced operator can usually detect a narcotic reaction during the first set of questions. Medication to reduce high blood pressure, to limit colonic motility (in ulcer patients), to relax muscle tension, and a hundred other ailments that perfectly innocent people have these days are also detectable in the first go-round. If you use a drug, or are under medication, you may make the test unusable, but you haven't beaten the machine. Your condition will be noticed and investigated.

All kinds of hypnotic and autohypnotic techniques have been dreamed up to beat the polygraph. Probably the only one that sometimes works is the use, in hypnotic trance, of the simple suggestion, "You will not betray yourself when answering any question!" Unfortunately for most subjects, this device is like most employed in hypnosis. It works in laboratory and hypothetical situations, where the subject is playing a game, but not in real and dangerous situations. Further, the subject who has real secrets to protect is usually so complex mentally and emotionally that hypnotizing him or her and crafting the proper posthypnotic suggestions are difficult and risky.

WHAT THE POLYGRAPH IS USED FOR

Personnel Security

It is a fact documented daily in the media that nations spy on one another, and the spies they use are one another's officials, when they can recruit them. One of the tasks of CI is to detect these penetrations and exploit them as weapons against their sponsors. Hence "personnel security." Hence reinvestigation of employees. Hence the polygraph.

A week or so after U.S. chief diplomat George Shultz uttered his famous threat to quit rather than to undergo a polygraph, the equally staunchly patriotic former diplomat Jeane Kirkpatrick wrote in her syndicated column, "Routine, government-wide use of polygraphs violates some basic tenets of liberal democracy. It requires that government employees prove they are innocent of wrongdoing. It requires they admit officials into private, even nonconscious, realms of feeling over which only totalitarian governments claim jurisdiction. It requires, in other words, that government employees give up basic rights of American citizens as a condition of employment."

What Kirkpatrick says is largely true. The polygraph, like all interrogation, intrudes on the subject's privacy. Whether that amounts to intrusion on his "basic rights" is a question with several sides. Most CI officers, who dislike *taking* a polygraph test as much as the next person, believe that being thoroughly investigated is one of the things a government officer signs on for when he takes his job, and most, especially those engaged in dangerous work, hope that their colleagues have been as thoroughly investigated as possible. It increases their own life. expectancy as well as that of their country. So they submit to being investigated themselves and to taking the polygraph. They do not believe that an immune elite class exists above a certain rank or among presidential appointees. It's a bit like the honorable tradition of the company commander eating in the enlisted men's mess and leading the bayonet charge when the time comes. If anybody in the Department of State is to be required to take the polygraph, the secretary of state (in this case a former U.S. Marine!) had damned well better take it, too.

And as for Kirkpatrick's precious privacy, believe me, the security officer has enough to do with real problems not to waste time on the sensitivities of her damp little soul. How many times have you been publicly humiliated, let alone black-mailed, by your doctor, your trash collector, your psychiatrist, your banker? Not often? Believe me, you are even safer with your overworked security officer and his polygraph operator.

Screening Applicants

When I want to plant a spy in another country's government, one of the things I do is train and document an agent to apply for a job in that government. When I want to keep another country from using that trick on me, I take a look at all the applicants for jobs in my government, and where the jobs provide access to secrets, I screen all the applicants carefully. One of my screens is the polygraph. Applicants are not required to take it. They can look for a job elsewhere.

In the United States, the polygraph works well as a prophylactic screening device for young people entering government for the first time. The average American, man or woman, fresh out of high school or college, has a strong sense of truth and falsehood, a strong sense of pride, and a healthy respect for machines like the polygraph. We call them good reactors. When we get a poor reactor, we investigate, and sometimes we get an interesting CI case, a chance to engage a real enemy and really earn our pay.

Case Support

Many CI investigations turn up a jumble of leads that is a mess to sort out. Once, for example, we found the KGB using a false Israeli flag, that is, pretending to represent the Israeli Service, to recruit Jewish refugees who had access to Allied secrets. At first, the recruited agents were asked to provide harmless information on Nazi war criminals, and then they were blackmailed to give Allied military information. A large number of Jewish refugees had made it to Britain, France, the United States, Canada, Australia, and New Zealand, where they joined up to fight the Nazis. After the war, many worked as investigators of war crimes. So at the beginning, the list of persons who might have been approached by the KGB under its false flag, and who might have provided information on what the KGB was doing, was huge.

In a situation like this, the polygraph can be of help. Most of the suspects have totally clear consciences and quickly volunteer to take the polygraph. Some learn to their surprise that they have been assessed ("vetted") by enemy agents without realizing it. And the tiny few who have been recruited by your adversary stick in the bottom of your sieve, where you can recruit them and double them back.

Incidentally, there is often an unexpected spin-off from polygraph programs like this. You may turn up a terrorist or narcotic connection not previously suspected. You may find a Czech where you were looking for a Hungarian. Or you may find an undiagnosed heart condition in a subject and have the satisfaction of sending him or her off to a doctor.

Personal Assessment

Your most important task in handling an agent or a double agent is to be able to predict his or her behavior. One of your tools for this is the polygraph. You can give him psychometric tests like the Wechsler-Bellevue, you can have his handwriting analyzed, you can investigage his background from A to Z; but for direct understanding of how his mind works, nothing beats the polygraph—not as a lie detector, but as an indicator of where he sits in his environment. *How* he lies and *how* he tells the truth are much more important than *whether* he lies. You should know by now that everybody lies. How and why are what count.

"Do you believe in God?"

"Did Mao understand Lenin?"

"Do Hungarians play better football (soccer) than Italians?"

"Is your wife unfaithful to you?"

"Does the Buddha in your household shrine have magic powers?"

These questions do not make a liar or a truthteller of your subject—they give you windows into his or her mind. As you get to know your subject, you can devise whole batteries of questions. Just don't use up all his adrenalin.

Recruiting and Testing Double Agents

When "turning" or "doubling back" a spy you have caught, your first task is to clamp control on him and keep it there. Your second task is to continually assess him, so that you can predict his actions in the situations you anticipate and get wind of those situations you haven't expected. From what we have said elsewhere in this chapter, you can see that the polygraph is one of your most useful tools for both these tasks.

When "playing a dangle" (running a provocation), control, you hope, is less of a problem. Your man or woman is yours from the beginning. But remember the emotional strain on any double agent, however loyal. Use the polygraph to test him and to diagnose his personal problems. Watch for problems of money, sex, and anxiety.

In all double agentry (and all agentry, too), use the polygraph only as an adjunct to your other tools. Do *not* fob off onto a "lie detector" test the responsibility for assessing your agent.

HOW THE POLYGRAPH IS MISUSED

The polygraph is misused when it is used as simply a lie detector. A symptom of misuse are two phrases heard from the lips of collectors and covert action operators: "passed the poly" or "flunked the poly." These case officers have abrogated their responsibility; they have delegated *operational security* to a technician. They have used the polygraph as a crutch, as a means to evade *handling* their agent. They should resign, drown themselves, enter a monastery, get the bloody hell out of the spy business, or go into journalism.

Unemployment among polygraph operators is not rampant. There are more jobs to be done than operators to do them. The result is a pool of poorly trained, inexperienced polygraph operators. And the further results are errors, mistakes, undetected failures. The prospect envisioned by a government policy of polygraphing all personnel cleared for classified material is a prospect of chaos. The job cannot possibly be done properly with the number of competent polygraph operators available. The amount of misleading and dangerous information that such a policy would produce is enough to nullify all the other security work the U.S. government can get done.

Meanwhile, the competent polygraph operators needed for sophisticated CI—where the real work is done—will not increase, because the competent operators will be drafted for screening and reinvestigation and for training neophytes.

It is a gloomy prospect. But for you CI officers who will be using polygraph machines and their operators to supplement your work, I say, find the best operators you can get, hold on to them, and use them wisely.

HOW TO MANAGE PHYSICAL SURVEILLANCE

Surveillance, the job of following and observing designated persons without being noticed, is intrinsic to counterintelligence. CI has so many uses for surveillance that I recommend no CI officer be promoted into management who has not himself been a surveillant on the streets and who has not run a surveillance team. The CI manager handicaps himself and weakens his organization when he disdains or fails to engage in surveillance.

Surveillance, by definition, is intrusion into the affairs of other people. If it violates their civil rights, you have yet another version of the CI officer's legal and ethical problem—not much different from that of a soldier in combat whose duty is to break the Mosaic Sixth Commandment, which forbids killing.

You cannot escape the ethical problem by choosing to specialize in analytical detection. Even when you are off the streets analyzing information, you will depend on the results of surveillance as much as on all the other CI techniques that snoop into the activities and personalities of private citizens.

LOCAL CONDITIONS

The basics of surveillance are the same everywhere, but practical conditions vary from region to region and from place to place.

How you organize and manage your surveillance teams will depend on some of the following conditions.

At Home or Abroad?

A law enforcement agency working in its own country may appear to have an easier job than a CI unit working under cover on foreign soil. Cover at home is easier to set up, accidental compromises are easier to seal off, the number of hostile personnel working against you may be smaller, and the pool from which you recruit surveillance agents is easier to vet (investigate and clear) because it consists of your own citizens. On the other hand, in a city like London, New York, Paris, Munich, or Milan, because of the size of the population and the freedom of movement residents of democracies have, local services sometimes feel overwhelmed by the amount of terrain they have to cover.

On foreign soil your job, though complicated, is often smaller because the CI targets are fewer. Unlike a home service, you do not have responsibility for investigating every hiccup and sneeze of the conspiracy that goes on around you. Your targets are limited by the size and shape of your CI program, and that is limited in part by the size of the surveillance mechanism you can deploy as well as by your charter.

Staffers or Agents?

Whether at home or abroad, you will probably have to use two different kinds of personnel for surveillance. Some special jobs require using only your own staff personnel, including yourself. This is expensive and it cuts severely into the other work of your unit. It is also inefficient, because your men and women who spend most of their time working on other matters cannot be expected to have the area knowledge, the practice, and the familiarity with cover that members of a full-time team have. But sometimes there are surveillance jobs that cannot be entrusted to people who are not sworn officials of your government. Such a scratch team of colleagues is fun to manage, because it is a game of friends, and more exciting than, say, a charades party or bridge tournament. You don't have to worry about penetrations, but you do have to worry more about accidents because you are using amateurs.

Less expensive and more efficient is the traditional surveillance team made up of agents. The members of the team, including its immediate chief, will not be staff officers, not be briefed on your program, and not be aware of your identity. They will be agents recruited and trained for their job of following and observing designated persons without being noticed. They will, in other words, be paid workers, like the crew of carpenters, electricians, and bricklayers that a building contractor hires and puts under the supervision of a foreman. They will not see the architect's blueprint of the house they are building except such portions of it as they need to see to do their part of the job. "Spitzels," "joes," "shnooks"—the slang names for these frontline soldiers are always patronizing, just like "dogface," "doughfoot," and "grunt" in the American army. But please remember that they are frontline soldiers, the ones who earn the medals for the likes of you.

The supervisor of the team will usually be an officer of your unit, fully cleared and briefed on your CI program. He or she will work closely with the team chief, being the link between the team and your unit, and may be known to its members, preferably by an alias.

Talent or Training?

Just as some people are quicker than others to pick up a language, some have more talent in surveillance—tailing a target. When you, or your team chief, are recruiting your team, you are like a director auditioning actors for a play. Obviously talent is what you look for first, remembering that the capacity to be trained is the most important talent. Throw away any notion you have from the movies and detective stories of the wizard-like lone wolf who can stick on somebody's tail for days on end and never get "made" (recognized as a surveillant). Such artists may exist, outside of my experience, but they aren't much use, because surveillance is a team game, where training and experience in teamwork are what count.

Surveillance is mostly a combination of area knowledge and common sense, reinforced by training and practice. Training and practice together amount to a lot of tedious rehearsal. Here are some hints on how to manage a surveillance team or tail squad.

COVER

The cover under which a surveillance team works should be detachable. That means that when one member of a team is compromised ("blown"), the other members can slip quickly away, like a snake shedding its skin, and leave nothing behind by which they can be traced. Sometimes what is left behind can be a "backstopped" cover—an office officially engaged in some other kind of investigation, which can simply refuse to comment on the compromised member. Sometimes it can be an empty office, a hole in the wall with a name and address printed on business cards, like "Air Pollution Research Committee." In a hostile environment, the cover has to be deeper—a messenger service, a taxicab company, a travel agency that actually performs the service it advertises and in which only a portion of the employees are members of the team, the others being unaware that their business is a cover.

Each cover must be unique, and no specific recipes can be given for establishing the cover of a surveillance team. Ingenuity and improvisation build cover at the beginning. Attention to security and tradecraft sustain it. If you do not set up adequate cover for your surveillance team, any effort to recruit and train members, much less use them, is wasted.

COMPARTMENTATION

How much do they need to know to do their job? The Rule of Need-to-Know, that famous rule of security, works best with robots on an assembly line. They have no human curiosity, no need to feel that their work is worthwhile, no human worries, and no human ambitions. CI officers, not being machines, are drilled and disciplined and encouraged to learn no more than they need to know to perform the task at hand, and yet they are also drilled and disciplined and encouraged to be curious, inquisitive, suspicious, and imaginative. The need-to-know principle is easy to formulate but hard to enforce—and especially hard to enforce on surveillance agents.

If you eavesdrop on a surveillance team relaxing over beer between stints on the street, you'll hear mainly speculation about the purpose of their current job, and about the lead that got them put onto it:

"Why are we tailing this guy? How did they get onto him?"

"Wiretap, obviously," says one, "and we're supposed to catch him filling a drop."

"Nope," says another, "they've got a double against him, that old man with the magazine under his arm that he met this afternoon."

By the Rule of Need-to-Know, the team shouldn't be talking this way. But talk it will, and sometimes you have to use a little deceit on your surveillance team. Often your reason for mounting a surveillance is a sensitive secret, such as information from a penetration or a double agent or an unsurfaced defector. You do not want it in the memory bank of someone, like a member of your team, who could be arrested or abducted and interrogated. So sometimes you have to give the team a *false* hint about why you have given them the job. If your lead did come from a wire tap, find a way to let the team think it came from a defector report. Say, "Our source just remembered a guy who lives at this address, but he doesn't know what he does for a living. Be careful, our source says he's tailwise [trained to spot surveillance]."

Deceiving your buddies is a sticky business, especially in what is a dangerous business, but sometimes it's necessary. Console yourself with the thought that you are protecting your team members as much as you are protecting yourself. What they do not know cannot be used against them.

COMMUNICATIONS

The operative word in "surveillance team" is *team*. Coordination is critical, and coordination means communications. How do members of a surveillance communicate with other members, and how does the team chief control the team?

The Command Post

During a surveillance, the team chief is like an infantry platoon leader in combat. He or she must have all available information instantly, must make instant decisions, and his or her orders must be instantly received and understood by the team. The command post must therefore be able to monitor the surveillance continuously. This is not always easy when, for example, a pair of targets split and one part of the team rides a ferry beyond walkie-talkie range or disappears up the elevator of a tall building, while the other part finds itself parked in a cafe. Choosing where to locate the command post is always partly guesswork (in a safe house, in a taxi, in a hotel lobby, in a delivery van, in a helicopter?). You have to compromise between what you have available (helicopters? vans? not today, sorry) and where you guess your target will go (out on the lake in a rowboat? over to the Ritz for high tea?).

Sentinel Points

If you have hunted crows in an American forest, you may have noticed that every flock of crows has a sentinel who posts himself in a tree where he can watch the terrain below and call out signals to the other crows in the flock. If you can spot the sentinel and shoot him first, the other crows will not fly away but stay exposed to your rifle. If you miss the sentinel, he will warn the others and off they go. Every surveillance team should have its sentinels posted during every surveillance, invisible to any rifleman.

One of my secretaries in a certain city used to complain when I took her away from her desk and put her at a pay phone with a pocketful of coins or on a park bench with a walkie-talkie hidden in her handbag. Her temporary job was to be a *sentinel point*, watching for countersurveillance and relaying messages between the people doing surveillance and the team chief's command post. She hated it. Another of my secretaries used to beg me to assign her to such work, because she liked getting away from the office. (The first is still a secretary; the second is now a senior CI officer.)

Sometimes the team chief can be his own sentinel point, but in a large surveillance, especially when there is more than one target and the targets are likely to split off in different directions, he will have to use subordinate sentinel points.

Telephone

Using pay phones to call the command post is an obvious way to communicate if you don't have to worry about telephone security, but in most parts of the world you do. A command post whose phone is likely to be monitored had better not use phones for communications, especially these days when so much telephone traffic actually goes by microwave or single-sideband radio.

Short-Range Radio

World War II gave us the walkie-talkie, which could transmit and receive for a distance of several miles, but could not be concealed in a pocket or handbag. The semiconductor chip and various improvements in antennas later produced small radios that could be hidden in a wallet or a hearing aid. Then came metal-coated balloons that could be put up over a city, when the wind was right, to reflect a high-frequency voice transmission from one side of town to the other. Still later came orbiting reflector satellites, which increased the range of small radios to just about any distance a spy would want. But the radio has not been devised that can select its receiver uniquely and evade interception. (Those which come closest to that goal are hideously expensive, far beyond the budget of the average surveillance team.) The security problem of radios in surveillance, therefore, is like that of telephones, magnified.

Intelligence stations, especially the hostile ones in our major cities, spend a lot of money and time monitoring the police frequencies and all those frequencies that carry surveillance traffic. Be aware of this when next you put a Soviet or Czech second secretary under surveillance.

One wonders how, nineteen hundred years before telephones or radios were invented, the surveillance teams used by the Imperial Roman CI service in the Roman Province of Palestine managed so well against the insurgency of Barabbas and the spies of the Parthian Empire. They must have relied heavily on hand signals.

Hand Signals

One of the several reasons that federal plain clothes detectives used to be notorious for always wearing hats was that the tilt of a hat can be a code—tilt to left, "keep away from me, I'm under cover"; tilt to right, "get reinforcements"; hat under arm, "meet me at the rendezvous," and so on. Two, three, or more surveillants working together have to have an inconspicuous system for signaling each other: Move ahead of the target, drop back, check in to the phone point, quit and go back to base, and the like. All kinds of props can be used, the more visible the better, so long as they are natural—handkerchiefs for blowing the nose or wiping the brow, pipes for lighting or knocking out or reaming with a pipe cleaner, eyeglasses for wiping, newspapers for rolling or carrying folded, handbags for women surveillants to carry by the strap or under the arm. Each team works out its own set of hand signals to fit the task at hand, then practices and rehearses; there must be a lot of practice and a lot of rehearsal. The hand signals used are more complicated and more numerous than those used by a catcher to a pitcher in American baseball.

Stakeouts

A few weeks ago in an American city, I happened to step into a newspaper kiosk for shelter from the wind while I lit my pipe. Standing behind the attendant, I noticed that he had a sort of log-book in front of him, and that he was watching a doorway across the street, which was the entrance of a haberdashery. When anybody entered the shop, the attendant made an entry on the log: "#7 IN 1417." When the same person came out, the entry was: "#7 OUT 1428." I had once gone into this haberdashery myself to buy some socks and had noticed that the prices on men's clothing were hugely above normal and that the volume of business done by the shop seemed very small. I bought no socks at the price demanded, and I was not astonished to read in the newspaper a few days later that the haberdashery had been raided by police and its staff arrested for dealing in narcotics. The newspaper kiosk had been a "stake-out," a "static" or "fixed" surveillance of a front for a narcotics dealership. The attendant was either a policeman under cover, or more likely a man recruited and paid by the police to watch the target of the investigation. If the target had been a suspected espionage live drop or safe house, the use of the kiosk would have been the same.

Sometimes a stakeout must be semimobile. Some of my old colleagues of another nationality will recall a case in a European city in which two Allied services worked together to confront and double back an enemy spy. We knew that he had left town to make a meeting with the enemy service but did not know when he would return. Our task was to surveil his residence without being noticed by his neighbors or by the local authorities. We managed to acquire use of a large residence a half mile from his house and then to mount from there a drifting surveillance by a sizable number of staff officers, men and women, who singly and in pairs casually strolled past his address each hour or so in different changes of clothing. About the third day of this time-consuming exercise, one of our girls saw him go into his house carrying his luggage, and within an hour we had recruited him.

Limpets

A car with a skilled driver is hard to follow through city traffic and is hard to follow on the open road without becoming conspicuous. Maybe it was the fish-and-game people who gave CI officers the idea of *limpets*. The rangers who study the migration and breeding habits of grizzly bears and other such elusive beasts use miniature battery-powered transmitters embedded in their hides after they have been tranquillized with a dart syringe. A vehicle does not submit to tranquillizing, but when unattended will accept a magnet to which is attached the same kind of beeping transmitter. The surveillance team with the proper small receiver need never come in sight of the target to follow it; indeed, the target can often be tracked on a map back in the office or safe house. The trick is to get inconspicuously near the vehicle for a few moments while you slap the limpet under a fender.

During the Cold War, in Soviet Bloc countries, the State Security Services made extensive use of limpets for surveillance, including some they contrived to attach to warm bodies. How? Well, think of your shoes, for example, that you just sent out for repair in Budapest—is the new heel hollow? Does the Alpenstock you bought in Prague for hiking radiate when you put it next to a frequency meter? Is there something funny sewn into the tail of your new Polish raincoat, the one you bought in order to be inconspicuous on the streets of Warsaw?

VEHICLES

Bicycles and helicopters and skateboards and scooterbikes and powerboats, as well as plain automobiles, can be used in surveillance. (I always wanted to use a blimp but didn't know how to get hold of one.) The one thing surveillance vehicles have in common is radio, short-range wireless communications.

Seldom is one vehicle enough, because in a surveillance of a target who is using a car, the tailing car is easy to spot, easy to evade—more so than a foot surveillant tailing a pedestrian target. So, as in foot surveillance, you have to have alternate tailing vehicles, and for that you need a fleet. Obviously every vehicle in your fleet must look different from all the others. The Toyota must be replaced at intervals by the Ford, which must give way to the Volvo (to fit your own area, substitute the commonest and least conspicuous models used there).

One vehicle must be the control car, the command post, with wireless communication not only with the vehicles in the fleet, and with whatever foot surveillants may be part of the caper, but with the supervising office. Often the control vehicle will also be the photo truck—that is, an ostensible delivery van, television repair truck, or the like—in which a small office can be concealed and which can be rigged for taking surreptitious photographs. These days most surveillance teams are organized around such a vehicle.

Arranging cover and documentation for surveillance vehicles may be the most onerous logistical chore you have. The principles and problems are the same as those that you encounter in setting up your support apparatus, discussed in chapter 4.

CAMERAS AND AUDIO GEAR

Often a team's task on the street is to get pictures of the people they are tailing or of objects like suspected dead drop sites and entrances to safe houses. A traditional and time-proven sneak-photo device is a woman's handbag, rigged to let her aim from under her arm so that the invisible aperture in the bag lets light into the lens of the camera in her bag when she activates the shutter by pressing an invisible button. A hundred other similar devices can be used: rucksacks, briefcases, bowling bags, tennis racket carriers, tobacco pouches, fur hats—whatever fits the cover of your team.

As for audio surveillance on the street, the concealed recorder is a standard device, though the number of times a team member can get that close to a significant conversation is small. I remember one occasion when a team member, close behind a target who was making frequent telephone calls from public booths, was able to get into an adjoining booth and intercept an operational message with a stethoscope applied to the intervening glass wall. We gave that chap a bonus for ingenuity beyond the call of duty.

WEAPONS

Members of a surveillance team tend to be cowboys. They get the habit from being simultaneously hound and hare, from taking risks every minute of the day. They like to be handy with a knife and a handgun, and to know a lot about judo, karate, kung fu, and whatever the fashionable name is today for such agile mayhem. Such handiness is occasionally useful in a surveillance team, but do not let your team carry handguns or knives. Why? Because the job of a surveillance team is to avoid trouble, and weapons will get it into trouble.

Exceptions? Of course: (1) A surveillance using law enforcement officers that may culminate in executive action (arrest and prosecution) requires the arresting officers to be armed. (2) An accidental encounter with violent criminals in a high-crime area, urban or rural, requires the team to protect itself. Even so, especially in cities, the best weapons are improvised: a tightly rolled magazine makes a good poking club (aim for the base of the nose); a twelve-inch wrecking bar, with the prying ends inconspicuously sharpened, makes a versatile weapon in the toolbox of a vehicle. Some French Resistance members in World War II became quite deadly with extra spokes from their bicycles, sharpened to be set quickly into a handle consisting of one of the rubber treads of a bike pedal. Alas, the age of the deadly hat pin is past, but I know of one mugger who departed his life of crime when stabbed through the underchin, tongue, roof of the mouth, and brain by the sharpened tip of a folded umbrella.

THE HALF-LIFE OF A SURVEILLANCE TEAM

Surveillance teams, like the engine in a car, wear out. Often when your car is old, you can tell that the engine is wearing out by its burning more oil and gas, overheating, stalling on hills, and so on. An aging surveillance team gives you no such warnings. In fact, it appears to get more efficient as it ages; and for the early part of its life, it does get more efficient. As the members of the team get experience in their techniques, learn each other's habits, and get to know their turf, they turn in a better and better performance. The part that you cannot see wearing out, but that does wear out as time goes on, is cover.

If you are working on foreign soil, the members of your surveillance team will usually be foreign nationals. Any small exposure of their cover, any accident that exposes them to the curiosity of local police or a hostile service, makes them vulnerable to recruitment. And when that happens, there goes the neighborhood, without your knowing it has happened. The next time you use your team for countersurveillance of a meeting with a double agent, your enemy (or maybe just a "friendly" but insecure police agency) now owns one of your operational secrets. And you don't know that you have lost it, which is a poor situation for a CI officer to be in.

The little accidents that erode a surveillance team's cover have an invisible cumulative effect, like metal fatigue in the wing of an old airplane. You often won't know about it until the wing falls off and your whole CI program crashes.

Such disasters have no cure, only prevention. Prevention requires making a ruthless decision to junk the plane before the wing falls off. The time to terminate a surveillance team is the point at which it seems to be doing its best work. Believe me, your administration and budget people will not like this decision. Everything they read of your reporting tells them to renew the project, avoid the expense of forming a new team and of pensioning off what to them looks like productive personnel. My advice is to insist on terminating the team, and to confront the administrative types with your superior operational experience and the fact of your command responsibility. When the controversy gets painful, console yourself with the thought that if they had any competence in operations, they would be in operations, not administration.

If your surveillance team is blown (compromised) and thus made useless (and you are lucky enough to find out about it), or if you wisely terminate it before the disaster, you have to have a backup. Again, your budget people will complain about the extra expense. But there is only one solution: For every surveillance team you have working, have another one in training, totally separate.

HOW TO MANAGE TECHNICAL
SURVEILLANCE

A more honest name for technical surveillance would be "electronic eavesdropping," or "taking sneaky pictures," but these terms make honest people uncomfortable. Samuel Morse's telegraph (1844), Alexander Graham Bell's telephone (1876), and George Eastman's roll film camera (1888) did a lot for the spy business, and even more for the counterintelligence business. Guglielmo Marconi's wireless (1901, in comfortable time for World War I) provided all that was needed to make secret communications and eavesdropping on them a major industry. Men and women sat with earphones on their heads and transcribed, transcribed, transcribed, making mistakes and missing groups. Then came (in World War II) the now-forgotten film recorder, which scratched intercepted signals and conversations onto movie film. Then came the magnetic wire recorder, also now forgotten. And finally came the tape recorder, now almost forgotten, and the cassette recorder, and (by no means the end) the digital recorder, with disk storage.

Bell's carbon-compression microphone was bulky—hard to hide in a sofa. Today's microphones, with transmitters built in, can almost be hidden in the lint you forget to wash out of your navel or in a cockroach. These days you never know where or when *Feind hört mit,* as the Germans say: *The enemy is listening.* Of course, if you have no enemies, you don't have to worry, because nobody but an enemy will go to the trouble of listening to, much less transcribing, what you sing to yourself in the shower. (Incidentally, the sound of running water is almost impossible to filter out of a recording; the shower bath is a good place to conduct your secret conversations.)

Transcription, that's the rub. Getting a tap just right on a phone, or drilling a pinhole for a microphone in a plaster wall, are sometimes frustrating and difficult, but they are a world of fun compared with "processing the take"—reducing hours of tape to a few meaningful typed lines in a report.

So, as manager of technical surveillance, you will put in a lot of planning time and make a lot of decisions on how to pick your targets. You will pick those targets whose activity is worth the enormous effort that goes into listening to and transcribing their endless trivial conversations in order to get that two minutes out of a week that mean something to your investigation. Or, if you are using surreptitious photography, you will limit it to targets whose activity is worth the endless hours of screening humdrum human activity on videotape for the five minutes when your target does something operational—or screening hundreds of prints from a still camera, usually blurred.

You will come to view with amused contempt that segment of the population that frets loudly about (they guess, fear, or hope) their phones being tapped, their bedrooms being bugged, or their pictures being taken on the street. Ah, the thrill of it, to think, or dream, that I am important enough to have my civil rights abused by *the Authorities!* Believe me, all you Walter Mittys out there who think I am prying into your private lives, I have better targets to snoop on, and those targets have better, or worse, things to be worried about than their civil rights.

REMEMBER THE SUPPORT FUNCTION

Of all technical surveillance, 73.92 percent (or make up your own percentage, so long as it is large) serves to produce leads for other kinds of surveillance and other kinds of investigation. Only a small proportion yields information that can be used in a report titled, say, *KGB Structure* or the *Terrorist Program of X Country.*

If you have to justify a tap or bug to a judge from whom you are seeking a court order or to a supervisor with a tight budget, be prepared to explain how simply getting a better line on some target, learning his habits, and finding out "what he has for breakfast" will advance your CI program. The judge may not understand this, being accustomed to favoring the kind of investigation that produces evidence to be used in court. The supervisor may be hungry for reports that he can disseminate and use to justify his budget. Neither may be generous toward what he may think of as low-level gumshoe work—unless, of course, she is the kind of professional who has done some gumshoe work herself. (Am I wrong to think that this kind of professional is becoming rarer at the executive level of our business?)

To sum up, the main purpose of surveillance, especially technical surveillance, is to support other investigation.

KNOW YOUR TECHNICIANS

Audio and photo technicians, collectively called "techs," are a weird and wonderful breed. They can incorporate things like beer cans into directional antennas, make invisible cameras out of wall switches, devise light-beam transmission circuits—in other words, solve all manner of technical problems by improvising gadgets you've never dreamt of. The problem you as manager will have with them is that they are so brimming over with ingenuity that they sometimes lose sight of the objective of an investigation and overcomplicate their job. "Art for art's sake" is the cliché used to label this tendency.

As manager, you can never hope to match your techs' knowledge of their trade, though you will want to run as hard as you can to catch up with them. Working with techs is one of the most enjoyable parts of a CI officer's job. Get to know them as well as you can.

TELEPHONE TAPS

Only a few professional spies, and even fewer professional intelligence officers, practice what they preach about telephone security. There is something intimate and insidious about a telephone call that has me making bloopers even when I know that my phone is tapped. I mention the real destination of a forthcoming trip or the real name of a contact that I am supposed to keep secret. Even worse, I try to use a private code—"seeing the banker," "going to the hospital"—when any eavesdropper who has been tapping me for a while knows that there is no banker and nobody sick in my family. I have provided his boss with a couple of leads.

But no matter how careful I am when using the telephone, I cannot help giving away information of value to somebody investigating me. For one thing, if I am obviously careful, I give away the fact that I suspect I am being watched. By merely using the phone, I give away the fact that I am home. By calling my bank, I give away an opportunity to investigate my bank account.

They are tedious to service, but telephone taps yield basic information on targets. They support other investigation. Here are some tips on how to manage them.

Central Taps

The easiest way to tap a phone, if you have the authority, is to arrange to intercept calls and record them at a central exchange. The procedure is automatic. Whenever circuits with designated numbers are active, one of your recorders at the central exchange tapes the conversation. When more than one circuit is active at once, several recorders work simultaneously.

You need authority to set up a tap at a central exchange. The police normally have such authority, or they can get it through the courts. The manager, as always, has the problem of security—can you trust the employees of the telephone company or national postal agency with whom you have to set up the system?

Local Lines

If you are abroad, you may not have the authority to tap telephones at a central exchange. You are then in the complicated business of gaining surreptitious access to a local line, maybe on the street, maybe through a sewer, maybe from an adjacent piece of real estate. Where the telephone line comes out of the wall, usually through a jack, is a fine place to tap it, if you can get at it. In any case you will have logistical and cover problems that can only be solved by ingenuity and improvisation on the spot. And then you'll have some technical problems: Do you tap directly and risk detection through a potentiometer at the exchange? Do you use an induction device (which can also sometimes be detected by its interference with the potential of the circuit)? To answer such questions, rely on the best wisdom of your techs.

The Telephone Bug

The mouthpiece of your phone is a microphone, and a very sensitive one. As you have noticed when calling home, it picks up the kids jabbering in the kitchen, the radio playing in the dining room, and the background conversation of whomever your spouse is having coffee with. When its signal is skillfully amplified, it is as good as almost any mike you could install in the room. Normally it only picks up sound when the receiver is off the hook, but in about a minute a tech with the screwdriver on his Swiss Army knife can alter it so that it transmits continuously over the circuit to the central switchboard or to a tap on the line between the phone and the switchboard. It is then both a tap and a bug.

The earpiece is also a microphone, because speakers and mikes have the same basic design. It can also be rigged to make a phone both tap and bug.

Your target can defend against the bugging function of this device by simply unplugging the instrument when he is not using it. But he cannot defend against an instrument which contains a concealed, battery-powered wireless transmitter, except by having his own techs check the instrument periodically. If he can do that, he is probably worth both tapping and bugging, because innocent targets do not have a squad of techs handy. On the other hand, he'll make *your* techs earn their pay.

HIDDEN MICROPHONES

American and British official jargon for eavesdropping with hidden microphones is "audiosurveillance," usually abbreviated "audio." In practice an "audio installation" is called a *bug*. Needless to say, this bit of slang lends itself to punning, especially in Britain.

The Monitor's Chore

If you collect oral history by recording interviews, you have noticed that your machine picks up and amplifies the rustling of paper, the striking of a match, the sound of an aircraft overhead, which the conversers do not notice. Yet the microphone will fail to get muttered phrases that the conversers understand clearly. If an openly placed microphone is limited in what it can pick up, a hidden one is even more limited. Unlike the human mind, a microphone cannot filter out irrelevant sound nor supply meaning through rational interpretation.

Monitoring and transcribing the take from a bug are therefore demanding chores. The monitor must strain to hear the words, playing portions over and over. He or she must speculate continuously about what communication is going on unheard—gestures, facial expressions, scribbled notes passed back and forth. The monitor must fight boredom and fatigue as hours go by without a word being uttered. Finally, the monitor must keep the kind of log that can be understood by an analyst and that can be easily collated with information from other sources.

Hard Wire

A hidden microphone connected to a receiver and recorder by a hidden wire probably delivers better sound than a radio transmitter. If you "control the real estate"—that is, if the room in which the mike is hidden is owned or rented or leased by you, while the targets are visitors to it—the job of planting the mike and hiding the wire is easy. So is setting up a secure listening post, because you can block off a room or an attic or use an adjacent apartment.

Most CI operations, however, happen on hostile real estate, especially when you are working on foreign soil. There, installing a bug will use most of the resources of your unit: safe house procurement for your monitoring point, construction of gadgets, and surveillance of the target to prepare for surreptitious entry and to protect your operational team when it goes in.

Wireless Transmitters

A hidden wireless transmitter radio with a microphone built in avoids some of the problems described above. There is no wire to hide and no adjacent apartment to rent, and the burglary part can go much more quickly—get in, plant the gadget, get out. Or you can hide the gadget in a table lamp, book, or picture frame and get it in "legally" through an ostensible repair person or meter reader.

But wireless transmitters have disadvantages. For example, they must have a reliable power supply, and batteries wear out. Sometimes they can be wired into the building's power supply, but doing that extends the time of your surreptitious entry.

Another disadvantage, very serious, is that wireless transmitters radiate. They send your signal out into the ether where it can be intercepted, and no reduction of the strength or frequency or direction of the signal can totally keep it from being intercepted. One of the Western services found itself once quite accidentally receiving sensitive intelligence from a bug installed by a Soviet Bloc security service in the office of a government official wrongly suspected of being disloyal to the communist government he served. For several months his dictations to his secretary were broadcast several hundred miles (on what the techs call a "bounce") into a receiver that was supposed to be hearing something much closer to home. That bounce, by the way, does not have to be a reflection against the Heaviside Layer of the Earth's ionosphere; accidents of terrain and architecture can cause a signal to bounce even when it is of so high a frequency that it pierces the Heaviside Layer and goes out into space where only Captain Kirk's *Enterprise* is supposed to glom onto it.

PHOTOGRAPHY THROUGH THE KEYHOLE

Banks use concealed still cameras to get periodic pictures of everybody in the lobby, and when somebody tries to rob a teller, he gets his picture taken. When you cash a check at an automatic teller, your picture goes into a file together with a copy of the check. The corridors, offices, and laboratories of institutions doing sensitive or dangerous work are monitored on television screens through hidden cameras. The police routinely run their "sting" (provocation) operations in houses or apartments equipped with hidden television cameras and sound equipment to get the goods (record the evidence) on persons enticed to negotiate criminal activity in the prepared real estate.

When you can control the real estate, surreptitious photography is easy. When, as on foreign soil, you are working on targets who control their own real estate, you will have to use all the tricks mentioned elsewhere in this book to make your installation, organize your monitoring, and set up your system of collation. Your support apparatus (see chapter 4) will get a complete workout. So will your file system (see chapters 16, 17, and 18).

MAIL INTERCEPT

Many countries run secret censorship programs on mail, both domestic and transfrontier. These programs are usually conducted by CI units masked as sections of the countries' postal systems. When working on foreign soil, you may or may not be able to arrange access to such official programs. If not, you are in the business of stealing mail, delivering it to your flaps-and-seals techs, who must open it, photograph it, and reseal it so that you can sneak it back into the target's mailbox without his or her knowing. Obviously, postal delivery persons and mail sorters become candidates for recruitment in any mail intercept operation. General-purpose support agents like hotel desk clerks, apartment house managers, and cops on the beat also can be useful.

COLLATING THE INFORMATION

As in all CI, the most important part of technical surveillance is collating the information (also see chapter 17 for much more on collation). Typically, such information is well suited to computer collation. The categories on which you collate the take from phone taps, for example, might be:

• *Target numbers:* the phones you are tapping.
• *Out-call numbers:* numbers called from target phones, recorded by the number of clicks dialed or the pitches of touch-tones.
• *Identities:* those known from automatic checking of all out-call numbers against a reverse phone book; those identified openly in conversation; those conjectured by monitor.
• *Message content:* usually designated by codes for what your monitor interprets as the *ostensible* content of the calls, for example, family, commercial, personal/social, operational double talk, and unknown.

A collation system covering months and years of phone taps can be a rich mine that yields a quantity of information on contacts. A master collation program combining the take from all technical surveillance with information from other CI operations can form the basis for many CI programs. I know of one collation job that enabled an imaginative counterespionage officer to contrive a deception program that damaged and nearly destroyed a hostile intelligence service.

DOUBLE AGENTS: WHAT THEY ARE GOOD FOR

No term is more misused by amateurs and greenhorns than "double agent." Once in the discussion preceding a routine polygraph test, I told a greenhorn operator that one of my specialties was running double agents and managing double agent cases. So young smartypants stuck a surprise question at the end of the first series, "Are you a double agent?" The breathing stylus on his machine jumped off the chart, and he had to write "Laugh" at the point of my answer. I then explained that the proper question would have been, "Are you a *penetration?*"

If you check the dictionary, you will probably find that a double agent is an agent working for two services at the same time. This will produce an image in your mind of somebody like Peter Lorre in the old movies, who spies on everybody and sells his information to the highest bidder. Today we'd call a double agent like that a "freelance," if we could find one. The fact is that since about 1945 the spy business has become a major international industry. Freelancers freelance just once. Then they either get gobbled up by professional services or (most often) they instantly go out of business. In other words, double agents, like all agents, are controlled by one service at a time. If control shifts from X to Y, a successful counterintelligence operation has been mounted by Y.

To a professional CI officer in an American, British, French, Russian, Chinese, Iranian, Argentinian, or any other service, "double agent" means one of two things: a *playback* or a *provocation*. And it means an *agent*, not a staff officer. To call Pyotr Semyonovich Popov (the subject of William Hood's totally authentic and factual book *Mole*) a double agent is to gabblegarble; Colonel Popov was our *penetration* of the GRU. If, when the KGB discovered that Popov had penetrated the GRU, it had doubled him back, kept him alive by providing intelligence of the quality he had been producing over the years, then he would have been a double of sorts (a "playback"). But in the case of Popov, as with most penetrations, the price would have been too high. They shot him. He was never a double agent.

CONTACT WITH THE ENEMY

An infantry unit commander will tell you that, whatever intelligence he is getting from the next echelon above, he feels out of control unless he has some contact with the enemy. When his front is quiet, he sends out patrols to scout the enemy lines, to draw fire, to grab a prisoner or two off the enemy's outpost line. He likes the red (enemy) side of his map to have something on it beyond what the topside chaps send down to him. He wants to have *contact with the enemy*.

The analogy between counterintelligence work and infantry combat is a pretty good one. As a CI officer, you have to have contact with the enemy. Organization charts of the enemy service, studies of modus operandi, and lists of identified enemy case officers are nice to have, but they don't give you much of a feel for the situation on the ground.

The basic use of double agents is to keep contact with the enemy. What you use that contact for depends on the state of your CI program at any moment. But without contact, there isn't much you can do.

THE PLAYBACK DOUBLE: THE CASE OF JANOS SZMOLKA

A *playback* is an agent of another, usually hostile, service whom you have detected and recruited ("turned") to continue his or her secret work under your control as a channel to and weapon against your opponent. Often, she has come to you after being pitched (approached for recruitment), has sought guidance, and has placed herself under your control at great personal sacrifice. Such a person was, is, Janos Szmolka.

The case of Janos Szmolka is in the public domain because a deputy chief of the U.S. Army Intelligence Command, then Brigadier General Charles F. Scanlon, testified about it to a Senate Committee. (The testimony is worth reading: *Hearings Before the Permanent Subcommittee on Investigations of the Committee on Governmental Affairs, United States Senate, Ninety-Ninth Congress,* First Session, 1985, 65–82.)

Janos Szmolka escaped from Hungary during the uprising of 1956, leaving his mother and a sister behind in Budapest. Instead of starting a Hungarian restaurant (of which we cannot have too many), he became a naturalized U.S. citizen, joined the army, and became a chief warrant officer in the Military Police (of which also we cannot have too many). He married a woman who was also in the U.S. Army, and of such women we cannot have too many.

Whenever he had the time, money, and official permission, Szmolka went back to Budapest to visit his mother and sister. They lived poorly, having against them the perennial suspicion of being enemies of the communist state because their son and brother Janos was a member of the army of the capitalist adversary. His visits came to the attention of the Hungarian State Security Service (often called AVH), their KGB, which made a business of (among other things) watching visitors from abroad and checking them out.

Szmolka got leave from his Criminal Investigation Detachment (CID) unit in Mainz for the Christmas holidays in 1977 and spent it with his mother in Budapest. There a friend of the family, who just happened to work in the Hungarian government, took him aside and said that another Hungarian government employee wanted to talk to him but did not wish to worry his mother, who should not be told of the meeting. In a restaurant named by the family friend, the friend's friend introduced himself as "Janos Perlaki" and bluntly made his recruitment pitch: His Service wanted Szmolka to steal military information on NATO and on the United States. In exchange, Perlaki would arrange "favorable" treatment for Szmolka's mother.

Oof. Put yourself in Szmolka's shoes. If you refuse to cooperate, your mother may receive not "favorable" but "unfavorable" treatment. You cannot again risk traveling to Hungary, and so you will never see your mother again. But if you do cooperate, you will be committing treason against your adopted country, against your unit, and against your wife, a fellow soldier.

CI officers reading this know that espionage for a hostile power is treason, a most sinful act condemned in Dante's Hell to the innermost circle with Judas Iscariot. But espionage induced by threat to a hostage puts the prospective agent in the quandary of choosing between what, in his mind, are two kinds of treason: betray your country or betray your family. Note a weakness, however, in the Soviet method: The agent coerced by hostage pressure will seek to wriggle out, to play both sides. In other words, hostage pressure is an inducement to double agentry. During the Cold War, we on the anti-Soviet side were proud of the fact that we did not use hostages for recruitment or control, but we couldn't make it work anyway. Our systems of government and our way of thinking didn't permit it, and I suppose that "weakness" is what we were really proud of.

C. W. O. Szmolka chose not to commit treason. He reported the incidents in Budapest to a competent CI Service in West Germany and placed himself under that service's control. From then on, that service (an element of the Defense Intelligence Agency) worked with him, in cooperation with other members of the American CI community, to get all possible information on the enemy while protecting him and his family.

The implied "unfavorable treatment" of Szmolka's mother had been the stick, as the Hungarians saw it, in his recruitment. The carrot was "favorable treatment," and to this was added money. In June 1978, when he drove to Budapest with his wife, he was contacted by Perlaki, who congratulated him on his decision to cooperate, promised him money in exchange for army documents to which he had access, and arranged for his mother to travel back with him for a visit in Mainz. The Hungarians were making it as easy as possible for him to make the transition to treason. The documents requested were harmless—training manuals on how to use the polygraph, unclassified legal directives, and so on. Their delivery would be a violation of regulations, but a minor one, possibly not worth a court martial, even if he was caught.

The game now became one of testing and probing on both sides. Our side had no further reason to meet the Hungarians on their own turf, and so we made it impossible for Szmolka to travel to Budapest. The Hungarians were timid about meeting him in Germany, and so, after arguing by mail and telephone for the next half year, they finally arranged to meet him in a third country. Meanwhile, his tour in Europe was coming to an end, and it seemed most advantageous to both sides for him to return to a stateside assignment at Fort Gordon, Georgia. Imagine how a Magyar case officer could strut and brag to his colleagues about having an agent in distant and exotic American Georgia, where incidentally was located the U.S. Army Signal School. Codes, you know. Ciphers, old chap.

So the meetings in the third country were tense and packed with operational work. Szmolka brought along the manuals and harmless documents the Hungarians had requested, and they took this as an indication that he was now hooked. Perlaki brought along a colleague, possibly his boss, who used the name "Vince Konc." They agreed to pay his mother a monthly stipend from Szmolka's own agent's salary, and again they promised generous pay for the information he would deliver. This time the information they wanted was not at all harmless: strategic defense plans, weapons, communications plans, nuclear capabilities, the locations of Pershing missile sites, cryptographic machines, NATO and U.S. war plans—a shopping list that Szmolka was to fulfill by flashing his CID credentials to get across security barriers and then using the copying gear that was part of his CID kit. He was too tactful to ask what these requirements had to do with the security of poor little Hungary, though they looked sort of Russian to him.

Now about communications. Ah yes, said the AVHers, we can meet you in Canada or Mexico, and if it's really important, we can meet you in the States. We'll tell you precisely where. Meanwhile, please memorize this recognition signal. And here is $3,000 in advance. We'll give you $20,000 for one of those U.S. Army cryptographic machines. And don't worry, we'll take care of your mother.

When Szmolka came back to the States, his case passed to the jurisdiction of the FBI per the charter of the National Security Act of 1947. In practice this policy meant that he often met two American handlers together—one from the Army, one from the FBI, and coins were flipped for who wrote the shared contact report that went into the central hopper at CIA. The objective of the operation now was to expose the enemy's assets in the United States.

The Hungarians were cautious. Szmolka explained to them through his postal channel that he was finding it hard to satisfy their requirements in the nonsensitive position to which he had been assigned. His CID badge wasn't all that magic when it came to getting access to Top Secret material, and this postal arrangement was clumsy. Why wouldn't they meet him in Mexico or Canada as they had promised?

But the Hungarians were stubborn. They had the Russian advisers looking over their shoulders pointing out that production to date had been flimsy. They wanted to see Szmolka again in Budapest. He responded that he couldn't risk the suspicion of American authorities by going yet again to communist Hungary. (In truth, his American handlers did not want to risk his life by sending him into the hands of Hungarian interrogators, who might at this juncture have decided to be harsh.) Finally a compromise was reached, and in March 1981 Szmolka flew to Western Europe to meet Perlaki and Konc in a third country. He took with him several rolls of microfilm that he had made at Fort Gordon under the close supervision of his American handlers. That microfilm did the trick.

The Hungarians now had some concrete production to show their Russian bosses—not a crypt system, to be sure, but some real photocopies of some real classified American documents. "Look, here's how they move their nuclear stuff through a city and guard against accidental spillage! Boy, the Soviet sabotage people will like that!" (Or whatever it was we provided them with. I am just guessing, but you can be sure it looked hotter than it was.) So Szmolka, Perlaki, and Konc all got stinking drunk together after the Hungarians had given him a new and better postal system and had specified meeting points in Atlanta and Augusta to which he was to bring documents on nuclear weapons and cryptographic systems.

Crunch. We could not afford to give away the poop the Hungarians now required. The Hungarians could not risk exposing their assets in the United States except for the sensitive material they had asked their agent to procure. For our side, there was not much choice. We had to "go to executive action" (a term misused in the press; it simply means arrest and prosecution). We'd have Szmolka signal that he has acquired an important item—maybe something cryptographic. Then we'd scarf up whoever came to the meeting and sweat him for whatever he knew.

And that's the way it went on April 17, 1982. The man who turned up and got into Szmolka's car at the meeting place in Augusta was Otto Attilla Gilbert, Hungarian born, U.S. naturalized. Unlike Szmolka, he had chosen the path of treason. The two exchanged passwords and satisfied each other that they were both who they were supposed to be. Szmolka handed Gilbert some classified material. Then Gilbert got out of the car and was arrested.

Gilbert knew quite a lot about the Hungarian intelligence service. When faced with the prospect of a very long prison term, he decided to tell it all. His plea bargain got him off with only a fifteen-year sentence. One wonders how much time he actually served before being paroled, but one can guess that there was enough time for us to do a thorough interrogation.

Was the price Gilbert paid for his treason greater than that paid by Szmolka for his loyalty? What happened to Szmolka's mother and sister? As you move into the field of double agent operations, you must expect some wounds to your conscience as you make the tough decisions over other people's lives.

DANGLES—CONTROLLED AND FREELANCE

A *provocation* is an agent deployed by you to be recruited by an opponent and to perform his or her secret work *under your control* as a channel to and weapon against your opponent. If Janos Szmolka had been deliberately sent to Budapest to dangle himself in front of the AVH (as the AVH and KGB now undoubtedly suspected), he would have been a provocation.

But beware the adventurer who tries to mount himself as a provocation, then comes to you with a ready-made double agent case. The breed is common, and its background for spy work is usually based on reading spy novels and watching TV.

I remember a woman whose hobby was sleeping with hostile intelligence officers. She was a nurse, librarian, schoolteacher, or something like that who kept getting jobs overseas in American military, diplomatic, or foreign aid installations. She could always dangle herself as a genuine American who knew a lot of other genuine Americans—including military officers, embassy officials, code clerks, and secretaries—and she could always say truthfully that she had a lonely sex life, because in fact she was not very attractive. Once shacked up with some Russian or Pole, she would report the contact to the nearest CI office, thus clearing herself of suspicion of being disloyal, and continue her sexual adventure under the "direction" of the CI office. The problem was that she was dumb—she was uneducable about the real spy business. She didn't and couldn't take direction, was too stupid, too preoccupied with her own vision of herself as Mata Hari. She was a nuisance and came to be a joke with all the services who knew her, communist, anticommunist, and neutral. She wasted a lot of time for everybody. I've forgotten what happened to her, but who cares?

LEVELS OF CONTACT WITH THE ENEMY

Level is a snobbish term, and it can mislead you. More likely, it can mislead your topside management. The first secretary of an embassy, if he is a spy service's agent, looks pretty high level, and if you have doubled him back against that spy service, you get credit in some quarters for the high *level* of your work. In fact, an underpaid code clerk who never gets invited to the embassy receptions is potentially more valuable as a spy than the diplomat. So may be the first secretary's assistant, who has a much better idea where classified material is filed than her boss. She has an inconspicuous private life in which it is much easier to communicate secretly with her. And she has an access to other assistants, code clerks, and potentially valuable "low-level" persons that her boss never dreams of.

Your topside management writes periodic reports to justify the allocation of resources, and those periodic reports are read by politicians and bureaucrats who view the CI business as they view a branch of the Ministry of Coal and Oil or a division of the Bureau of Statues and Monuments. They are impressed by first secretaries and not impressed by taxi drivers. The fact that the illiterate taxi driver whom you have recruited in Khartoum or Tegucigalpa is the KGB's key agent operating a surveillance team does not place him above the first secretary on the list shown to the politicians and bureaucrats who authorize your money. He is only higher on the list kept by *low-level* you.

You can be sure that your opponent in Khartoum or Tegucigalpa is not choosy about the *level* of his agents (though *his* topside management may be). Consider, for example, an operation of the KGB officer Oleg Lyalin, who worked in England. He recruited a clerk in that part of the bureaucracy of London that handles motor vehicle licenses. The agent, a Malayan named Sirioj Hysein Abdoolcader, was able to give the KGB lists of car registration documents and license plates that had been flagged in the files as not to be released to anyone asking about them, because they were used by the British Security Service (MI5) on surveillance vehicles. The lists gave the KGB a considerable advantage in the game of hare and hounds played by KGB case officers and MI5.

Like Lyalin, you had better not be choosy about the social level of your support agents. Flatter your doubled first secretary, milk him for what you can get, report his contacts with your opponent in your very best prose, but keep that cab-driver operation going. Maybe you'll find his surveillance team shadowing the first secretary's secretary.

ALLOCATION OF RESOURCES

They say that when the low-level worm got eaten by the high-level robin, it gradually got to feel like a robin. As part of the robin, the worm came to see eating worms as normal, moral, and efficient. So it will be with you when you find yourself part of that topside management that yesterday you resented so deeply. You now have the responsibility for allocating resources throughout an organization and among regions. You now must justify your decisions to the bureaucrats and politicians. Not only will you now suddenly become a little snobbish about *level*, but you will also find all double agent programs under challenge to prove their cost-effectiveness.

The budget challenge to double agent programs is very strong when your service happens to be rich with defectors and penetrations. Why, asks management, do we keep on with these low-level double agent cases when we have all this wonderful poop coming in from inside the enemy's fortress? Close the double agents down, the managers will say. Put their handlers to work at other things.

Such meat axing has occurred in the past. I'll cite no specific instances, but the result was bad and the meat axing was later regretted. The overly efficient managers had forgotten that defector information ages fast and that penetrations have a way of getting themselves killed. They found themselves alone, blind, and out of contact with the enemy.

DOUBLE AGENTS: HOW TO GET AND MAINTAIN A STABLE

The first purpose of any double agent program is to engage the enemy. Usually this means not only *enemies* but also potential and occasional *competitors*.

Not every intelligence service or police force that seeks to penetrate you is an enemy. When the Yanks tried to penetrate the Singapore Special Branch, and had their penetration doubled against them by Prime Minister Lee Quan Yew himself, they were not *enemies* of Singapore, and nobody in the Singaporean government thought so. But the Singaporeans ran a fine double agent case against them all the same. And so should you against whoever tries to put a worm in your apple.

Games are not worth playing for their own sake, of course, and when your adversary turns out to be a friend, the best thing to do is what the Singaporeans did—cork it off pronto, but not before having as much fun as possible at your adversary's expense. Sometimes you'll find your friendly adversary had a good reason—maybe he suspected a truly hostile penetration of your service and wanted to have a look at your security from inside. Maybe he was right. If he was wrong, slap his wrist hard. Then get on with your work against the common enemy.

The first and continuing task in any double agent program is to develop leads. The following investigation and planning that you hope will result in recruitments is the easy part of the exercise.

ASSESSING YOUR OPPONENTS

Assessing your enemy must start with assessing your own environment. Here are some questions to consider.

What Have You Got Worth Stealing?

If your environment includes a military unit, a nuclear research facility, an embassy, an intelligence office, a factory, or the planning office of a firm under contract to your government, then you'd better get busy making lists of what there is and where it is stored.

Who Wants to Steal It?

During the Cold War, the first answer to the question "Who wants to steal it?" always was "the intelligence services of the Soviet Bloc." After them, who else might have targeted your bailiwick? It depends on what there is to steal. The Dutch are probably not much interested in an Air Force base in the Caribbean, nor the Argentines in a naval base in the Indian Ocean, nor the Indians in a consulate in Auckland. If you find a genial Dutchman poking around operationally in Jamaica, look for a false flag—a Dutch flag flying on a Czech mast, for instance. In such a case, five minutes of conversation with the Dutch by your representatives in the Hague or in your own capital will get both services off to a nice start on a joint counterespionage operation.

On the other hand, you may expect the Dutch to be interested in anything to do with the former Dutch East Indies, that fifth-largest country in the world now called Indonesia, including adjacent areas: the Philippines, Malaysia, Singapore, and Australia. They may not mount any hostile operations against *you* in these areas, but don't count on it just because they are such nice guys. And don't get huffy if they do—their reasons are perfectly sound and no less moral than yours. Also, their intelligence officers are every bit as skillful as you.

Who Has the Tools for the Job?

A favorite number game to play with your legislature or parliament during the Cold War was to compare the number of Czech, Polish, Hungarian, Chinese, North Korean, North Vietnamese, Cuban, Romanian, Bulgarian, and Soviet diplomats (and identified intelligence officers) with the number of your own in any country. You were usually outnumbered, even when you counted your allies. Even the United States, with its FBI Intelligence Division, was outnumbered at home if you considered the *rezidenturas* targeting the United States from Ottawa and Mexico City along with those in Washington and New York's United Nations.

So one of the answers to "Who has the tools?" is the size and proximity of enemy official installations. A big installation means a big apparatus—lots of tools—safe houses, surveillance teams, letter drops, spotters, radio operators, handlers, and probably some reporting agents in place.

But if you happen to be isolated from the enemy official installations, then what? Well, you have a more interesting game: illegals or semi-illegals. This is awkward terminology that would not be necessary if the Soviets had been able to follow their own original concept of an illegal, a Soviet citizen who has adopted as cover the identity and nationality of another country. But the famous illegals have seldom been purely Soviet citizens, because they have had to live ("sustain cover") as non-Russians. The Russian Kolon Molodiy had lived four years of his childhood in California before becoming the Canadian Gordon Lonsdale. William Fischer lived from birth to age eighteen in England before becoming the Soviet colonel Rudolf Abel and being inserted into the refugee migration to America as Emil R. Goldfus. The Polish-born Ukrainian Leopold Trepper lived in Palestine and southern France before joining the GRU (from the Comintern) and being dispatched to Belgium as the Canadian Adam Mikler, later changing his identity to that of a Belgian named Jean Gilbert and extending his operations in Paris.

These days the job of operating an "illegal" *rezidentura* can be given to agents of any nationality, even those with natural cover in their own names. The foreign colony anywhere is a milieu into which enemy services work hard to insert their base chiefs. Because the illegal base chief's job is about 90 percent occupied with communicating by secret writing, by radio, and by courier, use your investigative facilities to develop leads to any kind of illicit communications. Then recruit a couple of deliberately low-level double agents to develop further information.

But, you say, detecting secret writing or microdots requires a mail intercept program, and that's illegal. Uh-huh. If you are working outside your own country, you may find that there it is not illegal; your host country may do it all the time. Furthermore, if you're working abroad, you are illegal yourself. Espionage and counterespionage are by definition acts of theft, against which there is usually a law. You have to get used to being a criminal outside your own country and to being paid for it.

At home, your job is to enforce the law. If that law forbids reading other people's mail, then quite simply you don't do it. But in most countries, there are provisions within the law for legitimate investigation by authorized agencies. Your outfit will have clear guidelines.

As for radio—wait until you are in place. You'll not be lacking for help.

Whom Have You Got Worth Recruiting?

To steal what you have, your adversary has to use people. He has to recruit agents with access. So the first question is, who has access to the list of sensitive information that you have already prepared? You have to go through the drudgery of copying rosters and making lists, and *do not* rely on the lists of people with security clearances that somebody else has assembled. These days, half the world has a security clearance, and the other half has access to what they are not cleared for.

Be consoled by the knowledge that your lists will be better and will have required less work than the same lists being put together by your adversary. He has to work harder to get the same information. Be further consoled that your lists can form the basis for a "dangle" (provocation) program.

Access to sensitive material is only one reason for enemy interest in your personnel. Remember the case of Oleg Tumanov, a twenty-one-year-old Russian sailor who jumped ship in November 1965, was routinely debriefed for the tiny amount of information he had, and was then given a job at Radio Liberty (RL) in Munich? Twenty years later, he disappeared from his job and shortly thereafter turned up in Moscow broadcasting anti-CIA propaganda. It's a fair guess that somewhere along the line he was recruited by the KGB, which has a whole sub-bureaucracy charged with disruption and destruction of anti-Soviet émigré organizations of the kind that RL and Radio Free Europe (RFE) depend on for talent. Destruction of the radios themselves was also a Soviet Bloc objective, and a sizable number of employees were recruited to plant bombs in restrooms, report on the lives of émigrés, and make grand exposés of RFE and RL as creatures of the evil old, murderous old CIA.

One hopes, humanely, that Tumanov found life in the USSR as free and comfortable as the life he had in Munich. The amount of sensitive information to which he had access in Munich that could have been used by the USSR against the United States or West Germany for military or political purposes is recorded, at KGB headquarters, on a single sheet of paper. It reads, "Radio Liberty and Radio Free Europe are American propaganda facilities located in West Germany. At one time they were administered by CIA. Their management has included, as Director, a former U.S. Army general and a former United States Senator. Their staff includes many persons who have escaped from our jurisdiction and are hostile to our form of government. The staffs of the radios do not have access to military, economic, technical or political information on the United States or West Germany. Agent Tumanov provided unclassified rosters and lists of the radio staffs."

The damage done by Tumanov was minimal, but the use to which he might have been put if he had been detected and turned would have been useful in a Western double agent program. Why? Because he could have reported on the techniques used for recruitment and handling by the KGB, and on their intentions: Which other employees were they looking over for recruitment? What kind of sabotage were they planning?

And especially, who was his KGB handler? This was important because the KGB routinely used émigré operations as a training exercise for junior case officers, and these often turned up later in more important roles. We needed to get them into the record early. (Maybe, in fact, the Germans or Americans had detected and turned Tumanov; maybe as a double agent he was useful; maybe it was an inkling of his having been turned that caused the KGB to withdraw him, using hostage pressure. I don't know, and don't want to know, because I have no need to know.)

So much for Tumanov. Bear in mind that the people in your bailiwick may not have access to sensitive material, but they do have access to others who have such access. They are potential "spotters" of potential agents. And never forget that an officer running a spy program for whatever service always needs support agents—accommodation addresses ("live drops"), couriers, "dead-drop" servicers (to empty the secret caches), surveillants, safe house keepers (to maintain what the Soviets called "conspiratorial dwellings" as meeting places and hideouts), strongarm men, and so on. Which of the people on your lists would qualify? Which are vulnerable?

What you do about vulnerability is discussed below under "Playbacks" and "Dangles." Suffice it here to say that you cannot and should not poke your nose into the private life of every person on your lists of people with access to intelligence. You'll ruin morale, get yourself a lot enemies, and fritter away a lot of time.

COLLATING LEADS

At home or abroad, you will always be short of manpower and time. The sure way to waste more of both is to neglect your study of leads, which also takes manpower and time. A rule of thumb in most situations is to budget one-third of your manpower and time to massaging the files for leads. Why, your management will ask, a whole third of everybody's time? Why not just a third or a half of the time of the chief and his or her staff? Can't they do all the paperwork and then give orders to the street people, who can then give full time to their street work? Answer: Maybe it works that way in a precinct police station (though I've not found it so in practice), but in a CI shop everybody has to be his or her own researcher, helped by the front office researchers, or details fall into the cracks, nuances get missed, cases go sour because of the inevitable unforeseen incident or the unavoidable accident. How often do we forget that even in the eight-foot-tall bureaucracy of our adversary, people oversleep, cables get lost, lightning strikes a power line, and *especially* the politicians trust their own judgment rather than the facts provided to them?

Furthermore, good double agent cases should be compartmented. Not everybody in the shop needs to know every case, and should not. That is the job of the chief and his or her staff. But because, despite compartmentation, two heads are better than one, the case officer has to participate in the research done by the front office on those cases he or she is working on. And the front office has to be attentive to the hunches and guesses of the case officer, who has a grasp of the case that the desk person cannot get, and who often has his or her life at risk.

Chapters 16 and 17 will discuss the mechanics of collation that both case officer and front office have to use.

PLAYBACKS

The assistant to the manager of the firm making custom chips for computers under contract to your Air Force may find that her new boyfriend is less interested in her personally than in her ability to work late at night next to the vault where your Air Force's technical specifications are kept. When he asks her to find out the combination of the vault, she may tumble to the fact that she has been tumbling with a spy.

What the assistant does next depends partly on how well the nearest security officer has done his job and partly on how well you, as a counterintelligence officer, have done yours. Does the assistant know where to go for help? Does she trust the security officers whom she will encounter to respect her privacy, to understand her personality, to protect her job and her personal safety? Does she think of security people as dumb flatfeet or as nice guys?

Nor should this example imply that women are more vulnerable than men. They aren't, by any means, and I could cite a few examples involving men of all ages that would weight the judgment the other way. I cite the hypothetical case of a female assistant because so often they have such fine access to sensitive information yet are ignored and set socially off to the fringes of their group by the management.

For your part, have you got a defined and mutually understood set of procedures with the security people to whom the woman (or man) will initially go? Do you and the security officers know each other personally and like each other? Is there resentment on either side over jurisdiction? Fights over turf are common in all bureaucracies, and this is a bureaucratic situation. The best arrangement is one in which it is taken for granted that the security officer is a CI officer who happens to be doing security, while the CI officer is a security officer who happens to be doing CI. This assumption is very near the truth of any CI or security situation, and indeed sometimes the same person wears both hats.

Work it out between you and get on with the operation: Recruit the assistant to be your double, investigate the hell out of her boyfriend, and handle her skillfully.

This is only a hypothetical (though not totally fictitious) example. The principles apply to all playback operations that start with a volunteer. To get the volunteer, you have to be set up for him—or her.

Security and Morale

Sometimes security and morale are in conflict. Nobody likes to think that some secret office with a lot of secret files and a lot of secretive people is secretly watching what you do. To be effective, a security organization has to have more than "good public relations." It has to be depended on for advice and comfort and help in all the problems that members of an organization have. Let me tell you a true story:

There was once in a sensitive agency of the U.S. government a competent and efficient secretary named Sue who was married to a chap named Fred outside the agency whose hobby was motorcycle racing. One weekend, at a big race at a big track in another state to which Sue had gone to watch her husband compete, Fred blew a rear tire while moving at about 110 miles an hour and smashed himself up—broken bones galore, including some vertebrae. Sue, who was distraught, telephoned her boss and told him what had happened, asking for emergency leave to get a motel room for herself and her two small children while she arranged Fred's surgery, hospitalization, and visits to him for several weeks. The boss, who was upset, called his agency's security office, said that the secretary held very high clearances and asked that she be looked after. This was a pretext, of course, because Sue with all her clearances was in no danger of leaking information from her motel room or from the hospital, or of being forced to do so by anybody nearby, and the security office understood this. Nevertheless, the security office sent a team to the city where Sue, Fred, and the two kids were stranded; arranged a loan from the credit union to cover emergency expenses; made contact with the local police; arranged for periodic look-ins on Fred in the hospital and Sue in the motel; set up a connection between Sue and the local pastor of her church; and notified Sue's boss the next day that all was as well as could be expected.

Was this a waste of the security office's funds and the taxpayers' money? No. It was a sound investment in morale and in confidence. It was *not* big brother watching, but little brother caring.

Manager Alertness

The security office played the role of little brother caring, but another key element in this true story was the boss caring. Call it "manager alertness." Here is a law of CI: The first, last, and essential security officer in any situation is the supervisor. As either a professional security officer or a CI officer, you must enforce this law.

The manager of the computer plant, mentioned above, whose secretary was asked by her boyfriend to be a spy, had not been doing his job if the girl did not come to him first with her problem. It was the manager who should have had her first confidence and should have worked with her and with the security officer. This is not the place for a lecture on personnel management, but it is a fact that many supervisors are afraid of their employees, especially women; hate to get involved with personnel problems (what do we have a personnel officer for?); and shy away from what might be viewed as meddling in other people's private lives. This diffidence or sloth may be acceptable in a brokerage firm or a Ministry of Mines and Milling, but in offices, agencies, or firms where enemy spy services are after your people, it won't do.

CI Informant Nets

The old-fashioned way of spreading a net for playback doubles was to set up a group of formally recruited secret informants. In Nazi Germany, the Gestapo found this system useful for all sorts of mind control, thought control, and population control that we rightly see as odious. Schoolchildren finked on their teachers for making jokes about Hitler, or they invented allegations to get rid of teachers who were too strict in marking homework. During the Cold war, the State Security Services of the Soviet Bloc (KGB et al.) used the same system, with a proportion of workers in a factory, say one in ten, coerced to report on the private acts of their comrades. This is a dirty business, and it misses the point of real CI.

The job of a CI officer is not to expose political beliefs but to engage alien intelligence organizations in clandestine combat. Your target is not agitators or polemicists but spies. During the Cold War, you would have found, when you got to know them, that professional Soviet Bloc intelligence officers were bored with ideology and found dealing with enthusiastic communists tedious. Their function, as they saw it, was to penetrate your government, and they interested themselves in peace marchers, antinuclear demonstrators, anti-interventionists, anti-whatever, or even in your indigenous Communist Party, only when those outfits provided a means of recruitment of individuals who could steal secrets from your government. To the degree that such outfits may constitute a recruitment pool for the enemy, they may be worth your time to penetrate with informants. But be warned that what your informants will give you will be mostly political persiflage. You may be using a vacuum cleaner where you need a pair of tweezers. On the whole, use tweezers.

Dangles

If you wait for the enemy to come to you, you may not know when he does. However trusted and admired your security organization may be generally in your bailiwick, its reception service may not be adequate to give you the contact with the enemy that you need. If the fish do not swim into your net, you have to give them a lure, a provocation, something that looks like a juicy worm but that has a hook in it.

How you bait the hook depends on where you are and when. You have to *assess your opponent,* as sketched earlier in this chapter, and tailor your operation to fit what you know or guess about that opponent's operations. You must select provocation agents with apparent or potential access to what the enemy wants, yet be careful always to be able to restrict that access plausibly if your dangle is recruited. You must make your dangle appear vulnerable to recruitment—drinking problem? money problem? family problem? shaky ideology?—but actually be invulnerable. Your dangle must have acting ability, nerve, and stamina. And he or she must have—what do you call that further essential quality?—integrity.

Setting up a dangle program is not made difficult by your enemy but by the crankiness of human nature, of the nature of the people you have to select, train, and manage. It is a frustrating activity, for both the agents and for you, because only a fraction of the people whom you have laboriously co-opted, coached, protected, and mothered will actually connect with the enemy.

When the operation finally closes out, be sure your double is properly rewarded. Security may preclude public recognition, but a commendation quietly conferred, a note of appreciation from the director or general or commanding officer, may help compensate for the troubles *you* have caused.

DOUBLE AGENTS:
FEEDING AND CARE

The man who keeps both a mistress and a wife is under a strain. He may get a peptic ulcer, develop high blood pressure, suffer insomnia, or take to drinking too much. His strain is much like that of a double agent, but a double agent's strain is increased by the fact that, usually, her life is at stake. If a philanderer makes a mistake, he messes up his living arrangements for awhile; if a double agent makes a mistake, she gets a bullet in the back of her neck.

And if a double agent's handler makes a mistake, it is the double agent who gets the bullet in the back of her neck. Double agents tend to keep this in mind.

EMOTIONAL DEPENDENCE

Feelings between a double agent and his or her handler are usually not affectionate. In the case of those that start with the detection and forcible turning of a hostile agent, they start out as hostile. In the case of those that result from a provocation program (dangles), they are routinely bureaucratic. In the case of volunteer playbacks, they are complicated by anxiety on the part of the volunteer.

But the nature of the relationship between a double agent of any kind and the case officer is such that emotional dependence is created on both sides. It may not be altogether friendly, but it cannot be altogether hostile, because the agent and his or her handler share a goal and work together solving problems, however reluctantly on either side.

This is somewhat like, but different from, the relationship between an employer and employee. It is different, for example, because the case officer may be a younger person with no visible social status or apparent affluence giving instructions to a highly paid and socially prominent senior official. Or he may be a mysterious figure who has suddenly appeared with power of life and death over a poor little spy in the attic of a ministry. He has a kind of authority, but it is only that of the member of a partnership who specializes in planning. He is not a boss. He lays out the plans, subject to his partner's concurrence, but it is the partner whose capital—that is, life—is at risk. Even in military agencies, where the case officer is a captain and the double agent a sergeant, there is a partnership that goes beyond relative rank.

The emotional dependence of a double agent on her handler is not only inevitable but essential to the handler's control of the operation. Those handlers who shrink from intimacy with a double agent because they don't much like her personally are not doing their job. At those times in your work of managing double agents when you get the feeling that the whole thing has turned into a soap opera, take a deep breath and play your role. It isn't soap you are selling in a double agent operation.

In many ways, the emotional relationship between a double agent and his case officer is like that between a subject and his interrogator, as discussed in chapter 5. This is partly true because so many double agent cases start with an interrogation, partly because interrogation is an element of the continuous testing of a double agent, and partly because a double agent has the normal human need to talk about his secret activity, yet has only his case officer to talk to.

Remember, though, that even if the agent whom you caught and turned was relieved to be caught and grateful to you for helping her expiate her guilt, she will still feel humiliated at having been caught. She may resent having to continue spying and may be careless. If she feels no guilt, her resentment will be even greater, and it will weaken her performance.

PHYSICAL DEPENDENCE

When you take charge of a double agent, you become responsible for his or her physical welfare, health, financial status, and safety. You can never control these matters totally, but you must help the agent control them with all your operational and administrative resources.

Health

Everyone's health is a mixture of mind, body, and emotions. Double agents have to work longer hours to do the extra work required of them by their enemy handlers and by you, and this hurts them both physically and mentally. They carry an abnormal load of anxiety and an abnormal load of suppressed anger. So they get sick—colitis (ulcers, gut cramps), high blood pressure, paranoid neurosis (they're out to get me), depression (crying fits, fantasies of suicide)—any of the diseases that psychiatrists call psychogenic or psychosomatic. The symptoms, which you must be the first to diagnose, are often heavy drinking, excessive use of tranquilizers, use of hard drugs, aggressive behavior in social situations (picking quarrels), or conspicuous withdrawal from social situations (sulking).

Financial Status

Not more than 96 percent of the world's adult population worries about money, unless it be 98 percent. If your double agent is within that percentage, you are obligated to arrange matters so that his work for you does not make him poorer, and preferably makes him a little richer. This point does not require much elaboration.

Safety

No job is more likely to generate dangerous enemies than that of a double agent, unless it be that of a member of the infantry. Provide your double agent with the spy business equivalent of entrenching tools, a good helmet and body armor, covering fire, and leadership. How you provide these elements of support will depend on your double agent's situation, especially as concerns his or her cover.

The Playback

The double agent who has volunteered, or turned to you for help and been persuaded to volunteer, is usually the easiest to support because he or she usually has a good cover for meeting you. You can usually contrive good pretexts to keep him out of harm and an inconspicuous method of compensating him for his trouble. The case of Janos Szmolka, discussed in chapter 9, is an example of the kind of playback in which you have good control of your own end of the operation. When it appeared that Szmolka's safety might be endangered by travel onto the enemy's Hungarian turf, his handlers found plausible reasons to prevent the trip.

When Szmolka got to feeling glum, as you can be sure he did from time to time, his handlers could meet him invisibly and comfortably and give him moral support. When he got to worrying about the effect of the operation on his career, his handlers could show him the glowing paragraph they had inserted into his efficiency report. When he needed some extra cash for a down payment on a car or a hi-fi set or a personal computer (I'm speculating, of course; I couldn't write this if I had read the file), his handlers could help him with a loan at the credit union or even with monetary payment beyond his salary. (But watch out for the income tax people; they have to be squared; you cannot conspire with a double agent to break a law of your own country.)

The Turned Agent on Your Turf

The double agent whom you have recruited by detecting his presence, then approached surreptitiously and persuaded to join your secret team—in other words, *turned*—and who operates in territory that you control, will be somewhat like a playback for purposes of support. The logistics of meeting, protecting, and paying will be comfortable. But the attitude of the double agent will be different. Because the operation begins with you and the double on unfriendly terms, you must expect him or her to resent your support. He may try to gouge you for money, and he may get deliberately careless in his tradecraft—in evading surveillance, in watching his tongue, in hiding incriminating material, and so on.

The Turned Agent off Your Turf

The turned double agent who works on alien turf will be difficult to support. He presents the same difficulties as the on-turf double—because his operation also started in a hostile situation. In addition he lives and works where you have few resources.

Example: A case already mentioned (chapter 6) was a woman agent detected and doubled against an Eastern European intelligence service. Her handlers would have preferred to keep her in the West, on their own turf. There they could safely play her through her radio and mail channel. But her parent service insisted that she periodically return to the communist capital for debriefing, testing, and training. Furthermore, she herself insisted on making these dangerous trips because her parent service owed her back salary that she was determined to collect.

It did not matter in her mind that her Western handlers would have been delighted to pay her a larger salary than the Easterners offered. We had no means of protecting her during these trips except to train her as well as we could to withstand the enemy's interrogation and to pass the enemy's tests. Fortunately, she developed rather friendly feelings toward us, possibly because we paid more attention to her personal problems and physical welfare than her communist handlers did.

She did fine. She completely buffaloed the enemy interrogators as she had not been able to bluff us, with our polygraph, and passed the enemy's tests well enough to get a raise in salary. I was never able to decide in my own mind whether her success was owing to her physical courage or to her own peculiar sense of financial ethics. Whichever it was (both?), she collected her pay from the enemy and she also collected valuable information for us. But if this double agent had been a convinced communist or had hated us for nonpolitical reasons, the operation might have failed.

TESTING

Testing a double agent is a continuous chore, a dull chore, and an essential chore. It begins, of course, with an exhaustive assessment. What makes him tick? Then, what will make him tick next time? As the case moves on, the main purpose of testing is to detect changes in the pattern previously recorded.

You must use several tools to test your double agents, and you must use all of them in concert. Let's look at the main ones.

Thorough Debriefing

Your double agent has no private life as far as you are concerned. He must have no secrets from you, and he must have total recall of everything that he does, hears, sees, smells, and dreams about while he is in your care. Why? Because you, not he, are the judge of which incidents may be relevant to the operation. You must therefore use an enormous amount of his time, and even more of your own, in recording *detail*.

Review of Production

Very important, of course, are the details of the double agent's contact with her enemy handlers. These should be recorded in the chronological section of the case file and collated with (1) other sections of the case file (legend, enemy requirements, build-up cleared, build-up passed, build-up pending clearance, etc.), and (2) the unit's dossiers (P-files) and files on groups and organizations (see chapter 16 on managing files). This material constitutes the double agent's *production*—her contribution to your service's knowledge of the enemy. As part of the testing, you will review and evaluate her production for conflicts with information from other sources and for internal consistency. Where obvious gaps occur, or obvious inaccuracies, you will speculate whether these are the fault of the double agent or the trick of an enemy who may suspect that their woman has been doubled or who may indeed be in control of her.

Personal Assessment

Not merely important but essential to your handling of the case is the information on the double agent himself. This you will meld into his own dossier, and you will review that dossier continuously. What you'll be looking for is any scrap of personal information indicating weakness or dishonesty and any tidbit that you can use in building his legend (cover story) to fit your management of the operation. How is he standing the pressure? Is his estranged wife about to turn up and make trouble? Is there an item in his past about which the enemy may learn that will change their handling of him?

Test Questions

Every meeting with a double agent should include at least one inconspicuous test question based on your study of the record of the case to date, as compiled in the files mentioned above. If the agent has neglected to report a fact that she should know and that you know from another source, find a way to bring up that fact in casual conversation. If she has reported a fact that you cannot check but that seems unlikely, pretend to have misunderstood what she said, and ask her a question based on what you think she should have said.

Formal Interrogation

Occasional formal interrogation by an outsider—an "inspector" or "visiting boss"—can be a useful test. It changes the atmosphere, breaks the pattern of the double's meetings with you, introduces an element of anxiety that you can pretend to shrug off as a bureaucratic nuisance. In every double operation that goes on for very long, the case officer gets into a kind of rut. His questions become mechanical, his thinking gets to be stereotyped, and he gets to taking things for granted. An outsider lets in some fresh air.

If your service uses the polygraph, you will obviously find it an enormous help in testing your double agent (see chapter 6). It may not detect lies, but it will give you a picture of your double's personality that will add to and modify your other information. If, however, you or your superiors view the polygraph as merely a lie detector for establishing the black and white of the double agent's reliability, don't waste time with it.

TERMINATION

"Disposal"

An ugly and inaccurate term used for the termination of a double agent case is "disposal." The double agent's handler and the handler's management view the agent as an "expended asset." From management's point of view, he or she should be gotten off the books as quickly as possible, should go away, should stop cluttering up the landscape, should be disposed of, as if in a trash compactor. How tiresome it is for the administrators that the double agent who is no longer productive still knows a couple of sensitive operational secrets, could blow (compromise) a case officer, blow a safe house, or shed unwelcome light on a counterintelligence program. Is he disgruntled? Will he write to his member of Congress, scream to the press, defect to the enemy?

This is the kind of attitude that gives the spy business a bad name. It also decreases the effectiveness of spy work. Let me tell you a true atrocity story that had a happy ending only because a couple of senior officers intervened in a "disposal" to counteract the administrative logic of managers.

An Atrocity Story

A young intelligence analyst in one of the American military agencies was approached under a false flag by Soviet intelligence. He instantly reported to a CI unit and was doubled back. Over the course of several years at different locations abroad and at home, the operation produced a quantity of valuable information on the Soviet service and many leads to other useful investigations. At times along the way, the man was in physical danger; his family life was disrupted; he was subjected to intense emotional pressure; and he contributed his own money and property to sustain the operation. Cash paid him by the enemy was automatically sequestered as evidence. He was transferred from place to place and from one part of the world to another at personal inconvenience.

The operation culminated in the arrest and conviction of two Soviet agents and the expulsion of a senior Soviet intelligence officer, who had been working under diplomatic cover. When the trials at which the double agent had testified were over and the enemy agents had been safely locked up, the military CI unit "disposed" of the man by firing him as a security risk, noting the fact that he had had contact with an entity hostile to his country and citing a regulation that all such persons were unemployable.

At this point senior officers of another agency intervened, recruited the man as an officer at a higher grade, and were pleased to watch him perform in a career that brought him to very senior rank and a position of high respect and affection among his colleagues in the interventionist agency. Happily, it can be reported that the top command of the military arm—which the military CI unit that had fired the man was supposed to serve—gradually recognized the arrogant, regulation-ridden, incompetent stupidity of that CI unit and caused it to be reorganized into a competent organization.

If you will be managing double agents or must manage their termination, I urge you to read the next section of this chapter carefully and take it to heart. Remember that operational thinking must *always* take precedence over administrative thinking.

Marriage and Divorce

The beginning of a double agent operation is a kind of marriage, and its ending is a kind of divorce. The traditional marriage service has phrases like, "For better or worse, for richer or poorer, in sickness and in health, till death us do part." It lost some of its meaning in the twentieth century as incompatibility became a ground for divorce. But most divorces, and all double agent terminations, include a "settlement," and most divorces do not end contact between the partners. Letters are exchanged about the welfare of the children, about money, and about other family matters. The family continues in altered form, sometimes quite comfortably.

The termination of a double agent operation should be like an amicable divorce. The settlement may include a formal secrecy agreement, a formal financial arrangement, an official letter of appreciation or commendation (which you usually must tuck back into the safe after its recipient has read it), an exchange of addresses and telephone numbers, and a friendly handshake. The double agent should always leave the operation with a feeling of pride in what he or she has done, even in those cases where it was done reluctantly. If you have done your job as case officer, both the agent and you will feel pride.

Transfer or Retirement?

Most double agent operations are of short range and limited duration. Terminating them means only arranging the double agent's resettlement. A playback can often be transferred to another assignment (if he or she is a government employee or soldier) or helped to move to a new position in a civilian trade. Some double agents, the big cases, have spent many years working for you and are in line for retirement.

DOUBLE AGENTS: PASSING INFORMATION TO THE ENEMY

A double agent operation is a channel in which information moves in both directions. On each end of the channel is an intelligence or counterintelligence service. The intelligence service seeks to ensure that the flow of material through the channel is beneficial to itself. The CI service seeks to ensure that the flow of material is detrimental to its opponent. Because of the need of both sides to keep testing and assessing the agent, most of the questions asked by the handlers on opposing sides are operational: "How does the agent acquire what he reports?" But the objective on both sides concerns substantive intelligence: "*What* has the agent reported?" An agent, or double agent, may pass every handler's operational test of reliability and skill, but his or her information must pass the consumer's tests of accuracy and relevance or the operation has no value. The handler must serve the consumer, or else his or her work is a waste of the government's money.

In service-to-service operations, those in which the targets are opposing intelligence services, the handlers are themselves the consumers of the (counter)intelligence. But even here they are subordinate to a higher echelon, often comprised of steely-eyed analysts, who are not about to be influenced either by an agent's charm or by the fun of the game. ("Game" = *Spiel*, the German jargon for a double agent case. We often speak of "playing" rather than "running" a double agent. And we speak of a double as being "in play," as chess players speak of the pieces on their board.)

The information that a service controlling a double agent passes to its adversary is unofficially called "snow," "smoke," "food-stuff," "chicken feed," and so on. Since computers began taking over the spy business along with everything else, it has often been called "garbage," as in "GIGO: garbage in, garbage out." Officially it is called "build-up." When the double is fully "built up" (accepted by the enemy), it may be called "deception."

THE DOCTRINE OF LAYERS

When I was a young case officer, I had several of the best coaches in the business of counterespionage, among them the Americans Jim Angleton, Bill Harvey, and Bill Hood, and some British chaps I cannot name. We found it useful to speak of *layers* of cover, visualizing the double agent game as one in which the dominant side could see more deeply through the various layers of apparent reality that constituted what could be known about a case. It was as if each double agent case was a canvas on which the surface picture was continuously being painted over, and the winning side was the one with the most sensitive X-ray machine, able to see the shape and detail of each layer from the surface down to the virgin canvas. An important part of each layer is the information—the build-up—that is fed into the channel by the double agent's handlers and that is, or should be, viewed with suspicion by the opposing handlers.

PASSING THE ENEMY'S TESTS

The compelling reason for never giving false information to the enemy until you are ready to practice major deception is that you never know how much the enemy already knows. His X-ray machine may detect a picture in a layer just under the one your X-ray machine is giving you. A parallel agent reporting to him from the same target as your double may give him a cross-check. A lost briefcase that you thought had been recovered before anybody could photograph its contents, a monitored indiscreet telephone conversation, an undetected bug in the target office—any such unknown circumstance could expose the information you pass as false. With build-up, you have to assume that the law first codified by Professor John L. Murphy will be in full force: "If it can go wrong, it will, even if it can't."

BALANCING COST AGAINST GAIN

The Szmolka case, discussed in chapter 9, may have had deception as its ultimate objective. Most double agent cases do, at least as a hopeful footnote in the plan. It never reached that objective, probably for two reasons: (1) It did not fit into any overall orchestrated deception program that may have been operative at the time, and (2) the *cost* in sensitive information that would have had to be paid to continue was higher than Szmolka's handlers were allowed to pay.

Szmolka, and his American handlers, had "built him up" in the judgment of his Magyar handlers to the point where continuance of the operation would have required passing the Magyars and their Soviet masters what they wanted—code and cipher material. This is the kind of stuff that cannot be faked, because it can be quickly tested. Conceivably, as in a fluid conventional battle situation, tactical cipher material can be passed for the purpose of short-range deception—"let them break the traffic of the units we are *not* using in the attack, and we'll use a different cipher system for the attacking units." But in practice such situations are rare, and Szmolka's "peacetime" case was not one of them. Furthermore, Smolka's handlers had to consider the fact that any information passed to an adversary increases that adversary's general knowledge and helps him, if only indirectly, in his espionage program to procure your systems.

A famous example of supporting build-up information at high cost is the case during World War II of an agent code named, by the Germans, Klatt. (His true name may have been Fritz Kauders, though some knew him as Richard Kauder.) He headed a special *Abwehrstelle* (German intelligence station) in Sofia, separate from the main station (*Kriegsorganisation Bulgarien*), whence he regularly transmitted accurate and valuable military information about Russian ground forces to Berlin (intercepted and deciphered, incidentally, by the British). The source of this information was a White Russian former British agent named Turkhul, who transmitted it to Sofia from a town on the Volga, where he allegedly ran penetrations of the Red Army command.

Actually, Turkhul was a controlled double agent of the Soviet service, and all his information was provided by the Soviets specifically for German consumption. In May 1942 Soviet forces under General Timoshenko mounted an offensive to retake the city of Kharkov and were defeated, taking huge casualties, mainly because Timoshenko's order of battle and battle plans had been betrayed to the Germans by the Russian CI service through Turkhul and Klatt. This sacrifice, as it would be called in chess, built German confidence in Klatt to the point that when he later provided false information—deception—on Soviet intentions and capabilities for defense of Stalingrad, the Germans acted on his information and suffered the defeat which was the turning point of the war. (Richard Kauder himself survived the war, settled down in Salzburg, and tried to eke out a living peddling his services to Allied intelligence units.)

THE BUREAUCRATIC PROBLEM

One doubts that any Western CI service would today be allowed to, or be willing to, sacrifice the "peacetime" equivalent of the 100,000 men and hundreds of tanks lost by General Timoshenko at Kharkov. That "peacetime" equivalent these days would be a weapons system—launching platform, propulsion vehicle, guidance system, warhead, the works. It would not be chicken feed. On the other hand, it would for damn sure build up your double agent. If the occasion should arise (it won't), give your double agent the code name "Clot."

The difficulties you have with build-up will start with getting the stuff cleared. You will not and should not have authority to give away your government's property, including its information, whether classified or not. Above you in the echelons of your service and of your government are officials who have *responsibility* for the government's property and for the government's secrets, and therefore only they have the *authority* to dispose of it. If this principle of law is not adhered to throughout government, then the government edifice gets termites in its beams and rafters, floors give way underfoot, the roof leaks, and eventually the walls fall in.

Clearance of build-up, therefore, requires bureaucracy. There must be clearance boards composed of those who do have the responsibility and therefore the authority. Military, political, scientific, technical, commercial, cryptological—your country may have secrets of each kind. And for each kind there must be a board, operating in utter secrecy, with authority to clear the information or equipment that you plan to give the enemy. That is a lot of secret bureaucracy, and you must not expect it to be either swift or efficient.

THE BUILD-UP LIBRARY

No double agent program can be effective without continuous reference to a library containing four kinds of material. ("Material" can consist of both written or sketched information and objects such as weapons, instruments, communications gear, and microchips.) The four kinds are

- Build-up cleared and banked for passage
- Build-up already passed
- Enemy requirements
- Material known to be lost

Keeping the Bank

Work through the clearance board to build a reservoir ("bank") of cleared material. Here you can take advantage of the tendency to overclassify information. One of the worst-kept secrets in the U.S. government is the fact that much material stamped SECRET is really CONFIDENTIAL, and much stamped CONFIDENTIAL should be handled OFFICIAL USE ONLY. Other governments, I think I can safely say, also overclassify their paper. You will therefore find much highly classified material that can actually be released without doing grave harm to your national security. This is vintage chicken feed.

But do not trust your own judgment when reviewing classified material, nor the first offhand judgment of a clearance board. Sometimes there are booby traps in an apparently harmless document. Usually these booby traps have to do with sources and methods—clues in the document to the means of its acquisition that may not be apparent to you or your clearance board at first glance. I can think of several valuable penetrations of Soviet Bloc governments whom the enemy detected and destroyed, as a part of routine damage assessment, by analyzing intelligence reports that had either passed through double agent channels or been acquired by espionage. The question asked in such an investigation is simple: Who had access to the stolen material? If the material is valuable—that is, sensitive—the list of suspects will be short. And so you need the analyst's equivalent of a mine detector when reviewing material for clearance, and your board should always be aware that it is working in a minefield.

Keeping the Record

Log, describe, index, and collate within the library each item passed, with careful attention to the time of passage. Let's look at the details involved here.

Enemy Requirements

"Requirements" is a name given to the tasks assigned by an intelligence service to its sources. Some American old-timers still use the term "EEIs"—"essential elements of information"—adapted from the procedures of military combat intelligence.

When a hostile service is developing a new agent, his task will be to steal anything to which he has access. When the enemy has broken him in and has him in a well-defined position of access, the agent will receive specific requirements, or sometimes a "shopping list" of all items his handler hopes he may be able to get his hands on. If you control him as your double agent, you will find that his requirements indicate what the enemy wants and, by deduction, what he does not want and therefore may already know. You must never take such a list from a single double agent too literally, of course, because some of her requirements may be designed to cross-check other of the enemy's sources and may not indicate what the enemy does not know. But with requirements from a number of double agents in your library, you can usually make accurate guesses. A master record of all requirements given by your adversary to all double agents must therefore be part of your library, collated with the other holdings.

Damage Reports

The damage report is a distasteful and tedious job that must follow every loss of information through a successful enemy operation, a breach of security, or a leak to the press by a politician or a public relations idiot (or a combination of these in the person of an incompetent executive). What has the enemy learned?

Some damage reports answer the question more fully than others. Obviously in cases like that of Kim Philby or Hans Felfe, who worked as KGB penetrations of their intelligence services (British and West German) for many years, the report can never be complete. But what can be known is useful to record because it can be collated with the other holdings in your library and used as collateral (see below).

THE USE OF COLLATERAL

"Collateral" is a technical term given to information acquired from a relatively *less* sensitive source that includes or duplicates information from a *more* sensitive source. An example of its use from Cold War days: You have an item from a penetration of the North Vietnamese government that you would like to disseminate widely, but cannot because of the high classification on all reports from your source. You know, however, that the North Vietnamese State Security Service (Bo Cong An), like all Satellite Services, is dominated by the KGB through what is called an advisory system. It may therefore happen that a defector from the KGB will know the item that you wish to disseminate. If you have such a defector, ask him about the item (without revealing your source). If he can report it, he has provided collateral. You can now disseminate the item broadly, attributing it to the Russian defector, and continue to conceal the existence of your North Vietnamese penetration.

By collating the information in your buildup library you, or your analysts, can form a picture (one of the layers under your X-ray machine) of what the enemy already knows. You can thus safely pass an item of build-up already put into one channel through another channel and further build up both channels in the enemy's mind.

MOLES IN THE ENEMY'S GARDEN:
YOUR BEST WEAPON

The British writer David Cornwell delights in coining names. For himself he coined the pen name "John le Carré," a translation from French of "Square John," meaning, in the slang of his time, a "square" (respectable and honest) "john" (patron of prostitutes). He preferred this to his own name, which could be taken to mean one who skillfully writes sentimental stuff, "corn."

Cornwell, alias le Carré, coined the term "mole" to mean a long-range, high-level *penetration* of a hostile intelligence service. The term had instant appeal among journalists and publishers, including the publisher (W. W. Norton & Company) of *Mole* by William Hood, who is an old professional and would never have used the term himself. "Mole" is a good metaphor— the little animal burrowing blindly among the radishes—and so has now entered the unofficial jargon of the spy business wherever spies speak English.

Hood's *Mole* remains the best publicly available description of a well-run *penetration* of an intelligence service—Pyotr Semyonovich Popov, a lieutenant colonel in the GRU. He worked for CIA in Vienna, Moscow, Berlin, and again Moscow before being detected and killed by the KGB. Other cases have been much written about by journalists and propagandists, but none of them has been chronicled with Hood's professional attention to what insiders call "tradecraft."

If the purpose of counterespionage is to manipulate enemy intelligence, as it is, then to have controlled agents in the staff of an enemy service is the most important objective of counterintelligence.

One bureaucratic point: To those intelligence collectors who think of CI as low-level gumshoe work, snooping and sneaking and peaking through keyholes, I say, ask yourselves who has better access and better cover to acquire sensitive military, technical, and political information than an intelligence or CI officer? Who holds the clearances? Who has the mobility? Who knows better how to send secret messages? Who knows better how to protect himself or herself?

As a CI officer, never forget that the absolutely best job you can do for your country is to develop and manage penetrations of hostile intelligence services. During the Cold War, you could be sure that your opponents in the Soviet Bloc had this as their primary mission. Not only Soviet enemies—remember the Ghanaian agent Sharon Scranage, who penetrated the CIA's Clandestine Service; the Chinese agent Larry Wu-Tai Chin, who penetrated CIA's foreign broadcast and translation service; the Israeli agent Jonathan Jay Pollard, who penetrated U.S. Naval intelligence; and the Dutch agent Joseph Sidney Petersen Jr., who penetrated the American National Security Agency. All these agents were citizens of the United States; their case officers were officials of governments not dominated by the Soviet Union.

STRATEGIC PLANNING

As with everything in espionage, and counterespionage, the best penetration operations are those planned and begun early, the *strategic* ones. The distinctions among *policy, strategy,* and *tactics* are useful here. *Policy* is a nation's intended course of action in its relations with other nations. *Strategy* is the deployment of all forces and all resources to implement policy. *Tactics* are the means by which strategy is executed.

In the spy business, policy is the selection of long-range targets against which espionage is to be conducted. Strategy is the recruitment and development of agents to steal information that will be needed at some time in the future. Tactics are the tradecraft of espionage and counterespionage that is used at every point in an operation.

The world masters of strategic espionage, as of chess, are the Russians. During the Soviet era, most "moles," whether known to the public or not, were early recruits who were carefully developed until they reached positions of authority and respect within the target organizations. Best known are the penetrations of the British services: Harold Adrian Russell ("Kim") Philby and Anthony Blunt, recruited at Cambridge University during the Spanish Civil War; and George Blake, probably recruited while studying Russian at Cambridge. A penetration of the West German service, Heinz Felfe, was recruited while unemployed and hungry in the postwar ruins of Dresden.

Take Heinz Felfe, for an example. He had been a sort of what people used to call a yuppie, a young upwardly mobile professional, in the Nazi Service (Reichssicherheitshauptamt, Abteilung VI, a component of the SS—Schutzstaffel) during World War II. Operating in occupied Holland, he liked wearing the uniform and taking salutes when he walked down the street exclaiming "Heil Hitler." He was also a good technician; he knew all the tricks of secret communications, interrogation, and case analysis. He had a brilliant future in the SS, until the end of the war ended the SS. By an accident he came from Dresden, a beautiful baroque city that had been destroyed near the end of the war by American bombing and that found itself part of Russian-occupied East Germany when the war ended. (For some of the flavor of that bombing, you might read Kurt

Vonnegut's *Slaughterhouse-Five* [New York: Delacorte Press, 1969]).

When Felfe came home to the ruins of Dresden, a Soviet intelligence officer gathered him in, fed him, and gave him a tour of those ruins. "See what the Americans have done. There were no military targets here. The Americans destroyed this monument to civilization because they have no feeling for art, no sense of history, only malice toward the best attributes of German culture. Help us fight these barbarians."

Felfe's grief for the death of his hometown was probably real enough in a man whose capacity for deep emotion was stunted from birth. But revenge was not his motive; nor did this ardent Nazi now become an ardent communist. He could be ardent about only one thing: his status as a clever operator. The communist system suited him as well as the Nazi system. Both were systematic. Ideology was not his motive, earlier, later, or at the end, back in East Germany, after he had been exchanged for eleven prisoners held in East German jails. He admired the professionalism and tradecraft of the KGB, and he especially liked the notion that a professional service should plan years, even decades, ahead to penetrate its potential enemies. There, he agreed with his KGB case officer, was a project in which he could do a job.

He made himself available to the nascent intelligence service of the new (West) German Federal Republic. That service became the Bundesnachrichtendienst (BND), headed by the former general Reinhard Gehlen and supported by the United States. The KGB had identified the United States as the "principal adversary" before the American citizenry had heard that there was a Cold War on. In the BND, with the invisible help of the KGB, Felfe rose to be chief of CI against that KGB.

Each one of these successful penetrations—Philby, Blunt, Blake, Felfe—was a strategic operation, begun with the recruitment of an agent when he merely showed promise of some day reaching a position of importance in an intelligence service.

Indeed, Felfe was recruited before the intelligence service that he eventually penetrated had even been organized.

HOW TO GET PENETRATIONS

The tricks and techniques for acquiring penetrations, sometimes called "defectors in place," are practically the same as for acquiring defectors. Much of this chapter therefore could be repeated in the next chapter, which will discuss defectors in detail. Please note that there are differences; not all volunteer penetrations wish to be evacuated at some future time, and not all volunteer defectors wish to or can be persuaded to work as spies before they leap the fence from their side to yours.

Russian Blackmail

The Soviet strategic moles discussed above were not blackmailed into being spies. Public records, however, chronicle hundreds of other cases, and the classified files thousands, in which the Soviet Bloc services have used or tried to use blackmail to recruit penetrations.

The tradition of blackmail in Russian espionage predates the Revolution of 1917. Several years before outbreak of war between the Russian and Austrian empires (World War I), the Tsarist intelligence service used a homosexual agent to entrap the chief of the Austrian service, the Evidenzbüro, and then blackmailed him into providing quantities of military information, including the Austrian mobilization plans. This Austrian spy, Colonel Alfred Redl, was careless in his personal behavior (boyfriends, gambling, alcohol) and attracted the suspicion of his deputy, Maximilian Ronge, who investigated him, exposed him, confronted him with his guilt, and then allowed him to shoot himself according to the code of honor used by the Imperial officers' corps. Ronge went on to head the Evidenzbüro throughout World War I, to found and command the intelligence service of the First Austrian Republic until the Anschluss in 1938, to live through World War II as a political prisoner of the Nazis, and to die quietly in Vienna at over the age of ninety. When discussing the Redl case with a young American CI officer in the year before his death, General Ronge often regretted that he had not interrogated Redl exhaustively. He repeatedly pointed out that the KUK (Kaiserlich and Königlich—Austrian Imperial and Royal) code of military honor simply did not permit such vulgar, expedient procedures. The young Major Ronge could not do what the old Emperor Franz Joseph would not have approved of. How different are our codes of honor now!

Western Inducement: All Penetrations Are Volunteers

The Western services try to use blackmail very seldom and almost always fail when they do. Oh, sure, there is an element of blackmail in any espionage operation, *after recruitment has occurred*, because the threat of exposure is always implicit. But the kind of blackmail to which the Soviets were addicted, like photographing people in the wrong bed, then threatening to circulate the pictures unless the bed-strayer turns spy, is not a common practice in the West. It does not produce enthusiastic agents, and most Western case officers lack enthusiasm for that kind of control.

A good spy for a Western service, and especially a good penetration of an intelligence service like those formerly found in the Soviet Bloc, must have his own reasons for betraying his organization. The task of the Western recruiter is to help him find those reasons.

Two Kinds of Volunteer

All penetrations volunteer for the job, but some do it when they already have a personal contact to whom they can apply, while others make their approach from a distance. It is the second kind of which we have public examples. Popov chucked a note into an American official's car in Vienna. Golenievski wrote an anonymous letter to the American ambassador in Switzerland. Oleg Penkovskiy walked openly into the American Embassy in Moscow, where he was rebuffed, then into the Canadian Embassy, again to be rebuffed, and finally made contact through a British businessman.

You'll not read much about how the other kind of volunteer gets to be a penetration, even when he eventually is evacuated and "surfaced" and comes to public attention. He is the one who is directly recruited by a personal contact. His recruitment gets no coverage by writers like David C. Martin, Chapman Pincher, Christopher Andrews, Thomas Powers, and Edward Jay Epstein, simply because the Western intelligence officers who make the recruitment are not identified to these types of historians and journalists. But all the same, his kind of recruitment is not rare.

ARRANGING THE FURNITURE

Whether you expect volunteers to walk in or to let you recruit them through personal contact, you have to be ready to handle them. This means a good support apparatus (see chapter 4), globally organized. Some of the facilities that you will require are the following.

Safe houses. When meetings can be arranged on friendly turf, safe houses must be prepared in advance. Volunteers who suddenly make contact must be taken to a secure place for debriefing and initial operational arrangements. Often this will entail an environment where a would-be defector can be persuaded to stay in place and be sent back to his or her post without the absence being noticed. After the operation is under way, safe houses should be established wherever in the world a meeting may be expected.

Brush meeting arrangements. In most penetration operations, frequent meetings in safe houses are not feasible. A "brush" contact, however, can often be arranged by which the agent can pass material or give a signal to an ostensible stranger in a public place. This trick was used over a dozen times in Moscow during the Penkovskiy operation. The wife of a British diplomat took her children to play in public parks so that Penkovskiy, ostensibly taking the air, could pass microfilm to her while appearing to be playing casually with her children. A more elaborate arrangement that I remember using required an agent to travel on weekends by rail from his headquarters, the internal security service, to his hometown. At a station en route, a train passed through in the opposite direction, so that for several minutes the two trains were stopped on opposite sides of the platform. During those minutes, the agent and his case officer, without speaking, exchanged identical briefcases, and then they rolled off in opposite directions.

Vehicles. Cars and drivers must be available to whisk you to a meeting, cart your agent to a safe house, or serve as meeting places themselves. On hostile or neutral soil, you will have to use rented cars or taxicabs, both of which require planning beforehand. Taxis are especially troublesome because you must plan to evade surveillance and driver curiosity by changing cabs several times, each time with a destination plausible to the driver. Remember that cab drivers are used to being questioned by the police; they have good memories and they often keep careful logs.

Portable tape recorders. Never rely on your scribbled notes of a meeting for an accurate record unless it is impossible for security reasons to carry a small recorder.

Portable quick-copy photo equipment. Be sure you have a compact kit of camera, copy stand, auxiliary light source, and extra film stored where you can grab it and move when you have a sudden meeting with a penetration agent. Such gear should always be available against the chance of a walk-in; if he is carrying documents containing information to establish his bona fides, you will want to copy them and let him take them back before they are missed. At the least, you'll want to photograph his identity papers.

Phone drops. To the potential penetration you are meeting socially, say: "Listen, Boris, don't call me at home. Here's a number that won't get either of us into trouble." To the recruited mole, say: "Here is a number to memorize and a code of signals for when you want a meeting, when you think you are under suspicion, when you have filled the dead drop (four rings, two-minute wait, four rings again)." These telephones should be set up and banked for *future* use; be prepared.

Surveillance. Your surveillance team, or whatever surveillance facilities you have to improvise, must cover meetings to detect signs of hostile surveillance of your agent or accidental surveillance of the meeting place by such third parties as the local police.

Dead drops. Never use the same dead drop twice. Those that you select must be inspected carefully, and those the agent selects must be checked out in advance by at least one innocent pass. If you cannot risk moving in the area more than once, leave the drop unemptied.

Live drops. A live drop who must be visited by the agent is a risky asset. Here, cover for the contact is all important. A live drop who is only an accommodation address (e.g., a British "letter box") is a detriment only because there are never enough of them. It is wise to recruit and maintain twice as many live drop accommodation addresses as you can foresee using.

RESEARCH AND TARGETING

Chapter 16 of this book discusses your file system, part of which are your *target files.* These are the compilation of all material from all sources that bears on the intelligence, CI, and other conspiratorial organizations that you are assigned to penetrate.

The files in your headquarters will probably be big ones, so that if you meet a member of a target organization at a diplomatic reception, or pick up his name through a double agent, or spot him through surveillance, and ask for traces from home, you should get a summary of his history as known from all sources.

One concrete example: I recall meeting an Eastern European diplomat socially whose passion for football (i.e., soccer) led him to discuss an international match that had occurred ten years before in another part of the world. Traces identified him as a State Security officer who had been sent to the match under cover of one of the coaches of his national team with the task of investigating the disappearance of one of his colleagues. The colleague had actually defected to the West and had provided a detailed breakdown of his service, including biographic information on the "diplomat" with whom I now found myself in contact. This information from the target file on the enemy service gave me an advantage over my new contact that proved useful. I judged that he would never volunteer and so did not try to recruit him, but I used my knowledge about him to protect another "diplomat" in his embassy whom we had recruited. That penetration was most grateful for my ability to coach him in evading investigation and was reassured that my service was, and is, professionally the equal of his own. The target files you maintain in the field and those in your headquarters must be your constant reference in your penetration program.

PLANTING THE SEED

Because you are a member of a Western intelligence service and of the community of Western services, potential volunteers already know that your service is one of the potential friends. What they may not know is where to go to volunteer. They need *access*, and if you are to give them access to you, you must contrive access to them. This will involve you in a game that often seems silly, between opposing intelligence officers at receptions and cocktail parties and laboriously contrived private meals, chatting about soccer and opera and fishing, each hoping to recruit the other, each returning to his office to write contact reports and extract into his files tidbits of biographic data or personal observation.

More often, the game is played by "access agents" on each side. The Hungarian trade attaché with whom you play bridge is probably reporting tidbits about you to your Hungarian opponent, and it does no harm if these tidbits give a picture of a sympathetic but loyal official of your government. If the Hungarian officer wishes, the trade attaché could arrange for him to drop by quietly as the third rubber is starting. Then begins the game of who recruits whom.

Sometimes your access to a target will come through a double agent channel. If an enemy case officer has been running a double against you, he can use that double to send you a message or set up a contact. Your embarrassment at being snookered through the double will be tempered by your pleasure at having a shot at number one in the side pocket.

MOTIVE: IS IDEOLOGY DEAD?

It is fashionable to refer to penetrations as "defectors in place." The theory is that somewhere inside their minds, these spies have "chosen freedom" and are working against the system in which they have been brought up and in which they have pursued their career to bring about victory for the system they have adopted and the destruction of the system they have abandoned. Their motives are supposed to be ideological.

Philby, the Communist of the 1930s

In the case of Kim Philby, the motive was explicitly ideological. He was a devout communist from, as he says, his last undergraduate term at Cambridge. "I left the university with a degree and with the conviction that my life must be devoted to communism" (My *Silent War,* London, 1968). But this was written under KGB direction after he settled in Moscow. For decades, he had devoted all his extraordinary skill in conspiracy and tradecraft to the *manipulation* of his friends and enemies. I submit that ideology may have been his door into his career as a manipulator, but his *motive* from birth to death was the satisfaction he derived from manipulation, and from the sneaky, smug act of betrayal itself. After betraying his country, his organization, his colleagues, and any number of agents, who lost their lives, he came to roost in Moscow, where he betrayed his only friend, Donald Maclean, by stealing Maclean's wife.

Felfe, the Nazi Turned Communist

In the case of Heinz Felfe, the motive was only accidentally ideological. He was a technician whose desire was to practice his technique as a member of what he took to be the winning team. Ideology bored him, except as a means of manipulating his enemies and his friends. The appetite for manipulation and for the self-gratifying act of betrayal was, as with Philby, the driving force of his life.

Philby and Felfe were not defectors in place. They had been defectors long before they were in place. If they were not motivated by ideology, and they weren't, what penetration is? I believe that, as a general rule subject to few exceptions, communist ideology was not the usual basic and real motive of effective penetration agents like Philby and Felfe that were run by Soviet Bloc intelligence services into those of the West.

Agee, the Unstable American

At first glance, the American Philip Agee is an exception to this general rule, but he really isn't. Agee served for twelve years in

CIA's Clandestine Service, working in Washington, Ecuador, Uruguay, and Mexico. He defected outright, probably before he had functioned very long as a Cuban penetration of CIA. Although he pictures himself as an ideological Marxist (*Inside the Company: CIA Diary* [New York: Stonehill, 1975], written with considerable help of the Cuban General Directorate of Intelligence), his former colleagues in CIA knew him as having been frustrated in his career, as disgruntled with his supervisors, and as a partner in a messy marriage long before he discovered that he was a Marxist. The fact that his Cuban/Russian case officers were not able to hold him in place as a penetration attests to his mental and emotional instability.

In my experience, Western penetrations into Soviet Bloc targets were also not motivated by ideology. Their motives were tactical, not strategic. They were bored with communist ideology, because everybody in the Soviet Bloc was bored with communist ideology. They volunteered to commit treason against their native communist system, or let themselves be recruited to do so, because they had some personal reason to sabotage their local bureaucracy.

During the Cold War, the general rule (call it a theory, if you like) that effective penetration agents were usually not motivated by communist *or* anticommunist ideology, was not fashionable on either side of the Iron Curtain. This will make your colleagues and supervisors who lobby for funds, conduct public relations, and run propaganda operations in addition to their clandestine work uncomfortable. I cite it because to bear it in mind will save you time and energy. The rule during Cold War days—which still applies today to similarly ideological adversaries—was that when planning a recruitment and in handling a penetration *of a Soviet Bloc–like service,* concentrate on your target's personal motives, not on his or her professed politics. If he wants to discuss ideology, by all means let him, but do not suppose that ideology is what really controls his actions, even if he thinks so himself.

Outside the arena of the East/West conflict, different rules may apply. Jonathan Jay Pollard's motive in spying for Israel may indeed have been ideological, even though Pollard was of unstable temperament. In operations to penetrate a terrorist organization, you will undoubtedly encounter a sincere, sometimes fanatical, temperamentally unstable ideology, possibly susceptible only to a false flag approach. That is, a member of the World Brotherhood for the Destruction of the Enemies of the True Faith may be more susceptible to an approach by somebody he thinks is a member of the Righteous Guardians of True Belief than by an agent of an official agency. If you manage to have penetrated the True Believers, you may be able to dog-leg or cushion-shoot into the True Faithers without your true flag showing. Or you may be able to invent a True Faith organization in order to use it to penetrate the True Believers.

WHO IS IN CHARGE?

Training courses in CI always emphasize the *control* of your agents, your double agents, your penetrations. *Direction* is a favorite word: "Always give detailed direction to your agent." *Training is* stressed: "Training of an agent must be continuous."

Yup. Very true, very sound. But in the case of a good penetration of a hostile intelligence service, control often rests with the penetration, not with you. Why? There are three reasons, having to do with what to steal, how to steal it, and how to deliver it.

What to Steal

Being a professional, and being in place, the penetration knows better than his case officer what the requirements should be. He knows, better than you, what his colleagues consider sensitive and important, what they most wish to protect from the likes of you. He therefore knows better than you what to steal.

How to Steal It

Being a professional, and being in place, the penetration knows better than you how to steal the material. Remember those silly Hungarians telling Szmolka (chapter 9) that he should use his Criminal Investigation Detachment credentials and investigative gear to photograph sensitive communications documents? If he had been under Hungarian control, he would have given his handlers a short course on how the U.S. Army really works. Criminal Investigation Detachment investigators do not get access to communications material.

How to Deliver It

Being a professional, and being in place, the penetration knows better than you how to communicate with you. He knows when and where he can travel; he knows what he can hide and where to hide it; he knows whether he is likely to be under surveillance.

WEAKNESSES

Does your professional mole always know that much? Yes, he usually does, but be wary all the same. In his choice of *what to steal,* he may do a little censoring. He may screen out items that might damage a personal friend, suppress things that might make him look incompetent or careless, and omit items that might cause you to give him tasks he does not want to perform. In his judgment of *how to steal,* he may use procedures known to his own service, and therefore vulnerable to detection, whereas you may have some procedures that would be more secure. In choosing *how to deliver*, he may improvise methods of communication and ignore the more practical apparatus of live and dead drops, phone drops, brush meetings, and the like that you may be able to activate.

Being a professional often has another disadvantage for a penetration: overconfidence. If your penetration is a good agent, it is because he is a competent professional, and competent professionals usually have a large quota of self-confidence. They also have confidence in the procedures with which they are familiar, those of their own service, and they tend to distrust those of an alien service like yours. They may not always be right.

MICHAL GOLENIEWSKI

An example of a professional who was in charge of his own operation was Michal Goleniewski, a colonel in the Polish State Security Service and a co-opted collaborator of the KGB. He reported to CIA through a mail channel that he set up, and through dead drops he arranged through his mail channel. He concealed his own identity from CIA until the time came for him to defect outright. Despite these evasions, his reporting exposed a number of very-well-placed KGB penetrations, including some mentioned in this book (Felfe, Blake, Molodiy/ Lonsdale), some mentioned in other public sources, and some still unpublicized.

Goleniewski was a competent clandestine intelligence officer who happened not to have the weaknesses cited above, or at least not fatally. An ironic fact worth pondering is that Goleniewski was insane. He believed himself to be, not Napoleon, but the Czarevich Aleksei, who would have been heir to the throne of the Romanovs if he had not been murdered on July 16, 1918, by the Bolsheviks. Whether his insanity contributed to or simply did not affect his skill as a clandestine operator is a question for all us sane operators to think about sometimes in the wee hours when sleep evades us.

TRAINING OR INDOCTRINATION?

To summarize the foregoing, a high-level penetration of a hostile service will consider himself to be in charge of your operation, and in practical terms, he will be in charge. That may weaken rather than strengthen the operation. Because you haven't much choice, you can only hope that your penetration is a truly competent professional clandestine operator or that circumstances let you train him.

Training the Amateur

If your penetration is not a clandestine operator but an analyst, an administrator, an executive, or (valuable but rare) a communicator, your problem in training him or her is mainly logistical. Can you meet him face to face in safe real estate? Then give him the full training course with all the tradecraft. If you must run him from a distance, hope that he has a quota of common sense, good powers of observation, and a strong sense of survival, because those traits are the essential ones that clandestine training and experience only supplement. Give him, from a distance, what tradecraft training you can by whatever means you can devise. And do not let the operation be run by a committee of your supervisors; in every good operation, the brass will want to horn in. Listen to their advice, but remember that while the brass gets the credit for successes, you get the blame for failures.

Indoctrinating the Professional

If your penetration is a clandestine operator (as most penetrations are because the others seldom survive), your job is not so much training as indoctrination. You must make him familiar with how your service does things, how your service looks at things, how your service feels about itself. At the beginning, your penetration will think he knows all that; he will expect you to react according to a picture he has in his mind, formed by years of looking at you through a haze of propaganda and fragmentary reports. He will expect you to perform feats that are beyond you, and will be astonished at some of the things you can actually do.

The key to successful indoctrination is *rapport*—the friendship, comradeship, and professional respect between agent and case officer. In the case of Pyotr Semyonovich Popov, CIA's penetration of the GRU chronicled in Bill Hood's *Mole*, the case officer maintained a rapport with the agent that was nearly as close as the case officer had with any of his American colleagues and that was closer than Popov had with any of his Russian colleagues. Identified by David C. Martin (*Wilderness of Mirrors* [New York: Harper & Row, 1980]) as one "George Kisvalter," and by Hood as "Gregory Domnin," he strongly resembled the Soviet premier Georgiy Malenkov, and he spoke equally good Russian. In Russian terms, he was a hell of a good guy. (In American terms, to speak for myself, he *is* a hell of a good guy.)

EVACUATION

Short is the life expectancy of any operation that penetrates a hostile intelligence service. You must realize this and do your utmost to extend the agent's life beyond the life of the operation. In other words, anticipate the day when your penetration becomes a defector, and plan with him exactly what actions to take on that day.

The signals that trigger an evacuation must usually come from the agent himself, because he is more likely to recognize the signs of danger than you are. If the CI or security elements of his organization are clumsy, he may detect surveillance, note a change of attitude toward him in his colleagues, find himself suddenly transferred to other duties, and hear of himself being investigated, or of material he has handled being analyzed unusually. At that point, it is up to the agent to pull the chain, to use the quickest means of communication he has to flush himself out of the operation.

Sometimes you, the case officer, and the whole team staffing the operation will get an indication that the operation is blown (compromised) or is about to be. Such an indication may come from another penetration, from a defector, or from a double agent. If your team is doing its file job properly, the indication may come from careful analysis of the case in the context of all you know from other sources. However you get that indication, move fast.

If you are skillful and lucky, the close of the operation will come under another heading: handling defectors (chapter 14). If you are unskillful or unlucky, you will have the blood of an agent on your hands. That is not only bad for the agent; it is bad for business.

DEFECTORS: YOUR
SECOND-BEST WEAPON

Next to penetrations (moles), defectors are your best weapon against alien intelligence services. They produce a much larger quantity of information, though the quality is obviously limited by the fact that their information is dated. Because defectors produce reams of information and because those reams can be processed with relatively little worry about protecting the source (the enemy knows you've got him; the enemy has a pretty good idea of what he can give you), you'll tend to feel a confidence in defectors, whenever you get them, that your professional caution withholds from penetrations and double agents. Your confidence will often be bolstered by affection. Here is a living body sleeping in your guest room, eating your food, and talking with you. Furthermore, he has joined up with you; he's on your side, he's a pal.

Beware. The fact that defectors are a productive and favorite source is not lost on the enemy. The basic rule of deception (see chapter 18), that you can usually make people believe what they want to believe, applies to sources as well as to information. Give your opponent an attractive defector, and what he has to say will be plausible. For that reason, during the Cold War, the mounting of bogus defectors by the Soviet Bloc services was a standard technique starting in the days of the KGB's parent, Lenin's and

Dzershinskiy's Cheka (All-Russian Extraordinary Commission for Combating Counterrevolution and Sabotage).

So before getting into the how-to of handling defectors, you might want to read up on some of the (inevitably controversial) cases that have been reported in the press. The KGB officer Yuri Ivanovich Nosenko, for example, was probably dispatched to deceive the American CIA about several important matters, such as the nature of the operational relationship between the KGB and Lee Harvey Oswald, who had assassinated President John F. Kennedy.

Another controversial case to ponder is that of the KGB officer Vitaliy Sergeyevich Yurchenko. In the pattern of many defectors, Yurchenko was emotionally unstable, estranged from his family, and involved in a messy sexual entanglement with the wife of a colleague. His defection in Italy appears to have been part of a private scheme to use the Americans to whom he defected to arrange his reunion with his beloved, who was stationed with her husband in Canada. He expected CIA to then arrange for the pair to elope back to the United States and live happily ever after on the bounty of his grateful hosts, to whom he would be providing priceless information and advice. The scheme went awry when the lady refused to defect. This rejection depressed Yurchenko, who thereupon used his professional skills to put himself back in contact with the KGB. The KGB used the redefection as if they had dispatched him in the first place—first with massive publicity accusing CIA of kidnapping, of torture, of malfeasance, of incompetence; and then withdrawal by the KGB to Russia for lengthy debriefing on all the personalities, installations, and intelligence requirements to which CIA had exposed him. After that? My guess is a bullet in the back of Yurchenko's neck, but he may have been given another role to play, just to confound KGB haters like me in the eyes of readers like you. This week, any week, when you read of defectors being "surfaced" (made available to the media), read between the lines of your newspaper and hope that your intelligence agencies are practicing counterintelligence while they hungrily debrief whichever defector has most recently arrived.

One more point: we are talking about real defectors, not refugees or commercial entrepreneurs. Tennis players, ballet dancers, dissident writers, and Zionists are not defectors as we use the term. By all means, let the immigration service welcome them all. We hope they get help and find a secure place in our society, but they are not material for CI reception, debriefing, and resettlement. That is, unless they have been sent as agents, in which case we'll get at them through our other operations.

INDUCEMENT

"Inducement" is the jargon used for persuading somebody to defect to you. It can be specific, as when you are in contact under some pretext with your target, or general, as when you merely arrange the furniture in such a way that the potential defector knows how to come to you when he or she decides to defect. The section of chapter 13 titled "How to Get Penetrations" (which are "defectors in place") applies directly to the defectors whom, for whatever reason, you cannot hold in place as moles.

ECHELONS OF HANDLING

Handling a defector whom you cannot send back as a penetration is somewhat like handling a prisoner of war in a combat situation. The prisoner captured on the battlefield must be interrogated in stages, at different levels of command, for different kinds of information. The regimental or brigade interrogation of prisoners of war (IPW) team, which gets first crack at the prisoner, wants immediate tactical information: heavy weapon locations, unit boundary lines, squad, platoon and company strengths, patrol and attack plans. When the prisoner gets back to

Division, the IPW team there wants unit identifications (Order of Battle), recent divisional movements, personal information on commanders, and (if the prisoner is a commander or staff officer) *tactical plans.* At this echelon of battlefield interrogation, the prisoner's level of knowledge is also defined. What does he know about strategic military matters? About political and economic matters in his country? About technical and scientific matters? Whether and how he is further interrogated at higher echelons depend on his level of knowledge. This may often not be related to his rank. A general's orderly may know almost as much as his general, and a lot more about some things.

Your defector from an enemy intelligence service must also be interrogated by stages and at different echelons. The first stage is a critical one and requires getting preliminary answers to five questions that will overlap each other in the asking.

First, does he need medical attention? Some defectors make their break in fairly violent ways and need a bandage or a splint. Some arrive intoxicated and have to be sobered up quickly so that the first stage of the interrogation can be quickly begun. All arrive in an acutely nervous state, feeling anger and fear. They may need tranquillizing, but only by a physician, if you can have one on hand, especially if your guy has alcohol in his system. It is very easy to kill or brain-damage a man if you use tranquillizers or sedatives indiscriminately.

Second, who is he, and what is he? Check out his answers immediately against available local records and flash a trace request to your home office. You'll get back a flash answer, and your colleagues back home won't in the least mind having been gotten out of bed to run the trace. How often do they get such a chance to earn their pay?

Third, how did he get here? You just know in detail his movements, acts, and observations from the night before the day in which he left his old place until he arrived at your place. Be alert as he recounts the story (over and over) for indications of fabrication, concealment, and distortion of motive.

Fourth, why did he defect? The English word "why" has two meanings that are frequently confused: reason and cause. Reasons may be ideological; causes never are. The driver for an enemy intelligence station who goes on a spree with a local prostitute, gets drunk, and cracks up his car has both a reason and a cause for defecting. The cause is the jam he is in; the reason, initially to avoid the consequences of his acts, but later he will probably find that his reason was to find freedom in the West. When his boss, a senior officer, comes to defect, he may have a reason of longer standing, but he will have a cause also, usually not much different in human terms from that of the driver. Job problems and family problems seem usually to be the cause of most defections at whatever level. So this question must be broken down into two subquestions.

What was the cause of his defection? What made him choose this moment, or what made this moment choose him?

What was the reason for his defection? At the beginning, he will usually have the *cause* uppermost in his mind. As time goes by, he will often discover that he had *a reason* and that it was ideological. He hated the Soviet system, he had chosen the democratic way of life, he wanted to help preserve freedom. Remember that all persons, including you, me, and your defector, like to believe that our decisions have been rational, that we had a logical and moral reason for whatever we have done. Otherwise we lose our most precious possession, our self-esteem. But remember that seldom in human affairs have decisions really been made rationally, logically, or morally. If, with any particular defector, you find that his decision was well thought out, deliberately planned, and morally tested, count yourself lucky to have found that rare artifact, an ideological defector. Handle it carefully, because it may crumble.

Fifth, is he genuine? A plant (phony defector, provocateur) is a valuable commodity. If you don't spot him as a plant, his value is to the enemy. If you do spot him, he is valuable to you as a counterespionage case, because whatever you can find out about the enemy's reasons for sending him to you will give you insight that may be of strategic importance. The information given to you by a phony defector is important, possibly more important, than that given by a genuine defector, for it is information the enemy wants you to have and therefore must be part of an enemy plan to manipulate your government.

Nosenko is a case to think about. He was a volunteer mole who carefully controlled (or the KGB controlled?) the meeting arrangements and means of communication for more than a year, during which he refused contact inside the USSR and repeatedly said that he would never defect outright, never publicly renounce his membership in the KGB or his Soviet citizenship. Then suddenly, less than two months after the assassination of John F. Kennedy, he reported that five years earlier he had personally handled the KGB's assessment of the future assassin Oswald in Moscow and knew that the KGB had never recruited Oswald. At the same time, Nosenko asked to be accepted as an outright defector, renouncing his citizenship and abandoning his family in Moscow.

Question: Why did the KGB want CIA to think Lee Harvey Oswald had never been a KGB agent?

Question: How much of the information provided by Nosenko on other matters had already been received from other sources? How much that was new could the KGB afford to throw away?

Question, question, question.

The Nosenko case has nearly all the questions you will need to ask when you get a defector from an alien intelligence service. Meanwhile, be prepared.

BE PREPARED

If you are not prepared to receive a defector when he arrives from wherever he has been, you'll not have much of a defection program. Being prepared for defectors overlaps arranging the furniture for penetrations (see chapter 13). Many of the same elements of your local support apparatus (see chapter 4) are used for both kinds of operation:

Safe Houses

Safe houses for reception of defectors should be arranged in echelons. Because any defector may be mounted against you specifically to uncover your facilities, or may be a low-level type who may change his mind after sobering up, the first safe house to which you bring a defector should be a throwaway, that is, one used for low-security meetings that may already be known to the enemy and to local authorities. When the initial debriefing is complete and you have decided that your defector is potentially valuable, the more secure and longer-range safe house to which you transfer the defector must be staffed with full-time caretakers, and the caretakers must function as guards, companions, and nursemaids. They must, in other words, be competent case officers, trained in agent handling and familiar with the case that they are handling. They should have a language in common with the defector, preferably his own, regardless of how well he speaks yours. They must maintain a journal recording his questions, remarks, and criticisms.

Portable Equipment

Portable equipment—recorders, cameras, and the like—should be available for use at the initial low-security safe house to which you first take defectors. The high-security safe house in which you begin your serious debriefing should be fully equipped with concealed recorders, cameras, closed-circuit TV monitors, secure radio and telephone communications to the base, and a defensive weapons system.

Interrogators and Polygraph Operators

Your first polygraph interrogation will probably be in your first, low-security safe house. An interrogation team of officers briefed on your defector's organization, supported by a polygraph operator, must be available around the clock whenever you expect a defector.

Psychological Assessment

The original psychological assessment of a defector must be made by the initial interrogation team and need not include professional psychologists or physicians. When serious debriefing begins, any support you can muster or have in reserve in the form of professional psychometrists, psychiatrists, and physicians should be committed. These pros can give you insight that you need when your defector is fresh and will save you, and him, any amount of later grief.

Surveillance

If one of your staffers—or a clerk, secretary, or driver—disappears, you go looking for him or her with all the means at your disposal. And when you find them, you try to bring them back. So, when you get a defector from another service, you can be sure that your opponents are making their best effort to find him and get him away from you. And if they can't get him back, they will try to kill him. Diligent use of surveillance on and around the safe house to detect signs of enemy surveillance or attempts at communication with your defector is an essential component of your defense. Remember also the case of the phony defector Vitaliy Yurchenko, who established his own secret communication with his *rezidentura* from inside a CIA safe house and used it to skedaddle back when it suited the enemy's purpose. Keep surveillance on your defector as well as on his surroundings. With an important defector, whether you suspect his bona fides or not, it does no harm to keep two levels of surveillance: one that he can detect and be aware of, and one that you hope he doesn't spot. I suspect that my former colleagues at CIA wish they had used this expensive trick on Yurchenko.

Vehicles, International Transportation, and Documents

Basic to all defector handling at whatever level is mobility. You have to be able to move the defector and all elements of the handling team quickly from safe house to safe house, from city to city, from country to country. If the clandestine logistics of your service are not capable of managing such movement, you had better consider turning your defector over to a friendly service and working the case jointly. In fact, joint exploitation of defectors among allied Western services is an established procedure and should occur in most cases, whatever the logistic arrangements may be. The only disadvantages are those discussed in the next chapter, under liaison—those of compartmentation and security.

RESETTLEMENT

Starting in the opening days of the Cold War, the steady flood of defectors from East to West made their resettlement a mini-industry within the mega-industry of Western intelligence. Because it is not a business that earns profits for its managers (all profit having already been realized), it is often viewed with irritation by the budget people, who like a bottom line with plus signs in front of the figures, whether those figures be in dollars, pounds, or marks, or in quantities of information. The result of this lamentable but understandable situation is that the budget people often find ways to skimp on resettlement of defectors.

They skimp, at least, after the original settlement, which was part of a legal contract. That settlement, an insurance policy, a paid annuity, a cash payment sensibly invested, will have been honored and vouchered to an account now closed and off the budgeter's books. What budgeters have difficulty fitting into their system is the continuing *operational* obligation of the service to its resettled defectors.

Please note once more that, with few exceptions, defectors are people who have difficulty adjusting to their environment, any environment. If they could not adjust to the environment into which they had been born and raised, we must not expect them to adjust with joy and gratitude to the alien environment—yours—to which they have defected. Please note, once more, that defectors are ideological and political in only that tiny part of their personalities that is ideological and political—the rest of them is human, conditioned by their childhood and by the world that will always be home to them, no matter what they have done or experienced later. When they have finished being debriefed, when they have contributed their last bit of advice, when they are pensioned off and discarded, odd foreigners speaking with a foreign accent and having no friends around them, they will have a rough time. They will be homesick, and this sickness is painful, sometimes even terminal if not treated.

They need help. But (the budgeters ask), because they have done their job, served out their usefulness, and gotten to the point where they can take their own chances and face their own problems like any other citizen of your country, why help them? There are two reasons. The *practical* reason is that they are a potential danger. For all their lives, they are targets of enemy recruitment. For all their lives, they have operational secrets of yours, which may age but never die. The *humane* reason for helping them is that they have *earned* your help. In our business, what is earned should be paid for, even if the payment is not specified in some "termination agreement." Otherwise, the spy business gets a bad name with the public and your spy service gets a bad name among spies, and you feel bad yourself because you have been a bad spy.

The best way to help a resettled defector is not to resettle him but to find him a job in the business at which he can work productively until his own aging tells him it is time to retire. A friend of mine, one of the earliest defectors from a Soviet Bloc service, liked to be called "Joe" because, after learning English, he found that in our slang he was a "joe." After his debriefing had been finished, he wanted to be an active agent. And so we did a little plastic surgery to change his appearance and documented him as an officer (actually several officers) of the service from which he had defected. For years, he moved with one or another of our case officers from place to place all over the world, recruiting officials of his former government under his former, now false, flag, and producing quantities of solid intelligence from their files. When we judged that his false-flag cover had about worn itself out, we gave him a routine official cover under which he handled agents for years, being a very good Joe. Finally came time for retirement, and so he retired, gray haired and contented, and he now putters among his roses, coaches his son's soccer team, or does what we all do in retirement. We never resettled him; we just helped him continue doing what he knew how to do: Spy.

Joe never wrote a book, but look at the books other defectors have written. They fill a long shelf in your service's training department. Never, never, never think of resettlement as disposal. No defector should ever be thought of as having been disposed of.

15

USING "FRIENDLY" SERVICES, FOREIGN AND DOMESTIC

The rule in all bureaucracies, whether military or civilian, whether a huge government agency or a small corporation, is that authority can be delegated but responsibility cannot—except in the business of counterintelligence. There, responsibility is delegated all the time through what is called liaison.

Liaison is one of the causes of peptic ulcers, high blood pressure, anxiety, depression, paranoid behavior, and bad dreams in CI executives. Every day, in liaison, they delegate the responsibility for the security of their operations to alien organizations over which they have no authority. Awareness of what this may mean causes worry. Hence the ulcers and so on.

Probably the closest and friendliest liaison arrangements since World War II are those among the English-speaking allies—Britain, the United States, Australia, New Zealand, and Canada. This tradition of friendly collaboration dates from World War I, when Sir William Wiseman, the British station head in Washington, worked closely with President Woodrow Wilson's Colonel Edward Mandell House, whose unofficial organization was the nearest thing the United States had to a central intelligence agency in that war.

An illustration of the tradition from World War II is the name of X-2, the CI element of the Office of Strategic Services

(OSS), the direct forebear of CIA. X-2 was christened after a British uncle, the Twenty Committee's coalition of services that collaborated in "double cross operations" (written XX, Roman "twenty," because typewriters had no cross; hence "X-2"). The Brits and the Yanks in their respective intelligence and CI services continue to refer to each other as "cousins" with the mixture of exasperation and affection that is common in many families.

But think for a moment of some names of British intelligence officers: Blake, Blunt, Philby, and add, with a question mark, Hollis. Through them flowed to the Soviet intelligence service the identities of American agents, the details of American operations, the names of suspects under American investigation—all acquired through liaison. Those Soviet penetrations of our cousins' services caused as much damage to the United States as to Britain. Would the damage have been less if the liaison had been less brotherly?

THE REASONS FOR LIAISON

The image of the British services riddled by Soviet agents like targets on a firing range might seem like an argument against liaison with those services. Indeed, because the British are not alone in being penetrated by the enemy, it may seem to be an argument against liaison of any kind with anybody. On the other hand, consider some peculiar geometry:

1. Blake, a Russian-controlled penetration of the British Service, betrayed an American-controlled penetration (Popov) of the GRU through information obtained by liaison with the Americans. Should the Americans have broken off liaison with the British?
2. Goleniewski, an American-controlled penetration of the Polish Service, betrayed

Blake to the Americans and British through
information obtained by liaison with the KGB.
Should the Russians have broken off liaison
with the Poles?
3. Michael Straight, an American citizen educated
in England who had defected in 1941 from
a position as agent for Soviet intelligence,
betrayed Blunt, a Russian-controlled penetration
of the British Security Service (MI5), to the
American FBI. But the FBI withheld the
information from its British liaison partner,
presumably out of distrust of MI5's security,
and MI5's investigation of the Blunt-(Hollis?)-
Burgess-Maclean-Philby complex was delayed.
Should the British have broken off liaison with
the American FBI?

In each of these cases, liaison continued. In each case, there was
a period of pain. Meetings were canceled, desks were shifted
around, procedures were altered, and unscheduled transfers
happened—but liaison continued. Why? Because it had to. Liaison is like Brer Rabbit's tar baby. Once you touch it, you are
stuck to it.

Liaison among services abroad is an extension of liaison
among services at home. The cause is the same for each: just as
criminals often move from one city to another, so spies cross
national borders. Unless the police of Munich and Wiesbaden
share information on a burglar who moves from one city to
the other, they weaken their chances of catching him. If a spy
who steals his secrets in Fort Monmouth, New Jersey, delivers them to a Soviet officer in Ottawa, both the FBI and the
Royal Canadian Mounted Police (RCMP) are well advised to
share information, perhaps run the case jointly. Indeed, they
will pool much of the general knowledge they acquire from all
their operations in order to improve the effectiveness of both

services. Further, both the RCMP and the FBI conduct liaison with the CI services of many other countries and with many other organs of their own governments.

At least that is how it works in theory, and that is how the theory is practiced. The cost in security, theoretically, is outweighed by the gain in efficiency. Possibly, in practice, the gain does outweigh the loss, despite the enemy's successes that we read about in our morning newspaper.

HOW LIAISON WORKS IN PRACTICE

Consider a simplified, hypothetical example of how liaison works:

1. A double agent in Sydney reports to his Australian case officer that his Czech case officer has given him an accommodation address in Toronto.
2. Through its liaison channel to the RCMP, the Australian Security Intelligence Organization (ASIO) requests a check on the address, without saying why the information is needed.
3. Through its liaison channel to the Toronto police, the RCMP requests a file check and investigation of the address, which turns up an apartment rented by a German businessman named Joachim Kramer, whose permanent address is in Hamburg. In the RCMP's headquarters files, the Toronto address is listed as one previously checked on a liaison request from the Malaysian security service. At Malaysian request, the RCMP has delayed putting "Kramer" under surveillance, taking for granted that the Malaysians do not wish to risk

alerting their target to the fact that somebody is interested in him.

4. The RCMP informs the ASIO that the address is registered to "Kramer," and that a permanent address is shown in Hamburg. The RCMP suggests a query to the German Bundesamt für Verfassungsschutz (BfV).

5. Through its liaison channel to the BfV in Cologne, the ASIO requests a check on the name and address in Hamburg.

6. Through its liaison channel to the Hamburg police, the BfV requests a check on the name and address. The Hamburg police reply, noting that this information has been requested and provided previously; the address is still a fire station, and there is still no record of Joachim Kramer. The BfV file check records a previous request from the Malaysian security service, with the Malaysian request that no action be taken to alert the target.

7. The BfV informs the ASIO that the address is that of a fire station and that there is no record of "Kramer" in Hamburg. It further notes that another *unidentified* foreign service has submitted an identical request. *Note:* According to the rules of liaison, the German BfV cannot identify the Malaysian security service as the previous tracer. To do so would be to betray the interest of a "third party," Malaysia, to the "first party," Australia. It can, however, note the coincidence for its own purposes, and although it is enjoined against putting surveillance on the address, you can be sure that the address will be kept on a running list of suspicious items and will be given special handling when

next it appears in traffic. *Note also:* The ASIO
has already run two risks, one in Canada, the
other in Germany; if a leak occurs indicating
CI interest in "Kramer" or in either of his
two addresses, the double agent operation is
compromised. *Note further:* The ASIO now has
CI information affecting the security of both
Canada and Germany. The ASIO must now
decide whether to risk further using its liaison
channels to develop the operation.

8. The ASIO, after taking a slug of Maalox, a
tranquillizer pill, and some medicine for high
blood pressure, decides to go fishing. It knows
from the BfV's reply that some other service—
a friendly one, because it is in liaison with the
BfV—has a piece of the same Czech operation
against which the ASIO is running a double.
It draws up a list of all the services known to
be in friendly contact with the Germans and
instructs its own liaison officers to mention
informally that the ASIO may have some useful
information on a Czech agent communications
system to share on a quid pro quo basis.

9. After a fair amount of sparring, a deal is struck
in Kuala Lumpur. The two services coyly reveal
to each other that they each have doubles
reporting to the same accommodation address in
Toronto, and they can then share information of
mutual interest, while protecting the identities
of their own double agents through code names
that they agree on as part of the deal.

10. Both cases proceed from that point. Eventually,
the Canadians may be brought in, because
recruitment of the letter drop in Toronto falls
within RCMP jurisdiction. The Germans may

also have a chance to participate, for investigation of "Kramer" will require support in Germany.

COOPERATION VERSUS COMPETITION

The foregoing example might lead us to think that liaison dominates the CI business. Not so. The four services mentioned—Australian, Canadian, German, and Malaysian—guard their own operations most jealously, as do all the others in the world. For one thing, elementary security requires that knowledge of sensitive information be limited to those who have a need to know; no Australian will ever come to think that any Canadian has a need to know about an Australian operation, except when exchange of *partial* information helps the Australian service.

Liaison relationships are like those between business competitors. All the restaurants in my hometown belong to a Restaurateurs' Association, which meets regularly to exchange information on such problems as processing of sales tax, credit card fraud, parking regulations, and police protection. Their cookery secrets remain secret.

Small services become accustomed to sorting out requests from different larger services and to using the differences to play one against the other. The Americans and the British, working in the same foreign capital city, keep their routine work secret from each other, yet both conduct liaison with the local service as well as with each other, and the local service comes to think that it knows more about each than they do about each other. Such confidence may be misplaced, however. I remember with pleasure the look of astonishment on the face of the chief of one such small local service when, at three in the morning, he was routed out of bed to face the British and American station chiefs standing shoulder to shoulder with a demand for assistance on a case they happened to be working jointly, of which he had never heard.

What does dominate the CI business, and therefore dominates liaison, is operational security (see chapter 1). The games you play in the name of liaison have that as the basic rule.

LIAISON AND PENETRATION

It used to be standard folklore that the primary and ultimate purpose of all liaison was penetration. Services were supposed to exchange information, and their officers were to socialize primarily for the purpose of recruiting one another. A friendly loan to an "opposite number" who was short of cash was supposed to move him toward being your paid agent. Rather squalid, eh? Also rather simple, and rather naive.

But think for a moment. When might one CI service have a reason to penetrate another with which it had a productive liaison going? There are at least three types of occasions.

Divergent National Policies

No two countries have identical foreign policies. Germany and Japan have divergent international trade policies, as do the United States and Canada. Sweden and France have divergent policies toward Indochina. India and the United States have divergent policies toward Pakistan. It follows that exchange of information through liaison channels, where such exist, will not be total. In such cases, CI services may seek to acquire the denied information by clandestine penetration.

The Pollard case is one in point. American and Israeli policies differ in their stance toward Islamic countries. The Israeli intelligence services have every reason to suspect that not all intelligence on Islamic countries collected by American intelligence is passed to Israel. If an opportunity arises, or can be created, to steal some of that denied information, the only thing that will stop such theft is the CI judgment of the likelihood of getting caught. Pollard got caught, and the American press and American politicians were noisily indignant that this little country of Israel, to which the United States had given so much money, would return such generosity by acting like Jean Valjean in Victor Hugo's novel *Les Misérables* and stealing the good priest's candlesticks.

Let such righteous indignation be reserved for the press and the politicians. It has no place in the thinking of a CI officer, who must work in the real world.

Future Changes in National Policy

Today's friends may be tomorrow's enemies. It is not so long since the British were aligned with the Russians against the French, and later with the Russians and the French against the Germans. The United States was hostile to France as recently as the period of Maximilian in Mexico, and toward Britain as recently as the American Civil War. Britain's Italian allies in World War I became Britain's enemies in World War II, and are now again allies in NATO.

But when a nation's foreign policy changes radically, the membership of its bureaucracy changes less and slowly. Old liaison relationships tend to survive, with obvious implications for penetration operations.

The Desire to Monitor

An investor with much of her capital tied up in a firm likes to know what goes on in that firm. She feels more secure if she has a member of the firm's management telling her how business goes from day to day, what executive decisions are being made, what the cash flow ledger looks like, and what the personnel problems are. So a CI service, whose capital is its information, sometimes likes to have a penetration in a liaison service in order to keep an eye on the internal workings of that service. You will feel this desire most strongly when you have reason to suspect that your partner service is penetrated or is practicing poor security.

The Itch to Meddle

I have never known a service that was satisfied with the way another service was being run. The closer the liaison relationship, the stronger is the urge to improve the management of the other service. Most attempts to influence the other people's management take the form of earnest advice, exhortation, and an exchange of think pieces. But sometimes you will succumb to the thought that if you only had your own person in there, you could make things better. But do be careful. Unless the liaison service you try to penetrate is so incompetent that it's not worth liaising with, it is probably good enough to catch you out, and when you get caught trying to recruit a friendly liaison partner, you will have one hell of a flap on your hands. The professionals in the target service may understand and grin a little, but (1) the target country's politicians, (2) your own politicians, and (3) the world press will be merciless. Liaison may even be suspended for a while.

HOW TO MANAGE FILES

Files for the counterintelligence officer are as much a part of life as the car he drives, the plane he flies, the feet he walks on. Without organized information, the CI officer can't get where she has to go. The CI officer is both the slave and master of his or her files. Accept this as a fact of life in the CI business: The structure of your files will be as essential to your effectiveness and to your safety as the design and construction of your car.

Files are not only folders, microfilm, or computer records— they are also the people who manage the information, collate it, research it. Especially you, yourself. I know a CI officer who is bored with paperwork, prides himself on being a street man, relies on hunches, and leaves the collation and research to a file clerk. That man is only half a CI officer. He will do himself and his organization a favor by shifting to a job in paramilitary operations or sports announcing. His job can be taken over by the file clerk, who, as it happens, wouldn't mind a chance to get out on the street, doesn't mind the smell of powder, and doesn't mind doing a complete job on a case.

CHRONOLOGICAL FILES

The basic CI file at a headquarters, a field office, or a home base is the chronological file, the "chrono," a collection, dating back as far as possible, of all reports that do or could contain CI information. It is organized chronologically *not* by what the librarians call "date of accession" but by "date of information," which is usually the date when the report was written.

A chrono file gets to be bulky, and the managers of real estate get cranky about the amount of space taken up by paper, microfilm, or disk storage by records that are seldom retrieved. "Why," they ask, "hold records for years, for decades, that pertain to defunct operations and dead persons? Let's purge everything older than three years, or at least thirty years." Professional CI officers call these managers "the neat and tidy people" (N&Tniks), and tempers flare between them, especially when budget-conscious executives support the N&Tniks.

Both sides have a point. A report from 1945 on the Rote Kapelle (the German code name for a Russian World War II espionage complex, usually translated "Red Orchestra"), or from 1948 from the salvaged files of the Shanghai Police or from 1975 on the structure of the Bo Cong An (the North Vietnamese version of the KGB) will seldom turn up in a search, twenty or forty years later, for the name of a member of the New People's Army in the Philippines. Is such a long shot worth the expense of maintaining a large historical holding?

Often the answer is yes. The original bulky file on the Rote Kapelle, now incorporated into the main system at Langley, Cologne, or Melbourne, if properly collated, may well show a connection between the Filipino's father and an agent who worked for the Soviet spymaster Sandor Rado in Switzerland in 1944. Much stranger things happen in the CI business every day. When does information become history?

So what can be done about bulk? Well, first remember that CI cannot be efficient in the same way that a publishing house is efficient. The cost per item of information stored and collated is not a measure of value of that item, nor is the frequency of its use comparable to the dollar sales of a book. Accept the fact that in your files full many a rose is born to blush unseen.

Lean, therefore, away from being too neat and tidy. Lean toward big files, old files, and well-collated files. Keep them big, let them age, and make them as neat and tidy as you can without destroying them. Use the latest technology, both to reduce bulk and to facilitate manipulation.

Some years after the end of World War II, the British Security Service (MI5) noted two facts: (1) Many of its most experienced personnel were reaching the age of retirement; and (2) the files in London were getting unmanageable, partly because of their bulk and partly because the maintenance procedures were obsolete. Obviously the people best qualified to purge, reorganize, and modernize MI5's file system were the ones being lost to the service through retirement. So MI5 began a program to bring back the old case officers and old analysts to work part time as file redressers. The retirees, if they wished, could earn a little money on top of their pensions, could use their special knowledge of old cases to winnow out the chaff, and could make changes they had always wanted to make in the system—all at relatively little cost to the Service. Furthermore, the old hands could solve some mysteries and generate some new cases that otherwise would have lain hidden in the old paper. Happily, this procedure has been copied elsewhere in the Western world.

INDEXING BY NAME

In the old days, the only indexing a report got was of the names in it. Battalions of file clerks worked from dawn to dusk reading reports and painstakingly extracting each name onto a 3-by-5-inch card that also recorded the title and date of the report. The cards were then filed alphabetically so that when you asked for a trace on a name that had come up in a case, a file clerk could get the whole report and give it to you to read.

Today the same process continues, except that the "carding" may be done at the console of a computer as an entry to a list stored on a CD or DVD, and the report may be on microfilm, microfiche, or on a CD or DVD. In the world's larger services, these days, most reports are written or transmitted electrically and so already exist in digital language, which can be indexed by computer software. Older, predigital reports, cables, memos, and the like may in some cases be read by optical scanners and thus translated into digital language for storage in computer files. A name trace, therefore, may well call up a printout rather than an original document, and much faster. The battalions of file clerks are being replaced by companies or platoons of console operators.

But the main category of information by which reports are retrieved in CI work is still "family name, middle initial, and given name," supported where possible by date/place of birth, location, name of father (in Asia), and dossier number (see below). The additional information lets the file clerk or the computer eliminate the John Smith, Kovacs Istvan, or Nguyen thi Mai that you are not looking for. A couple of yards of 3-by-5 cards all labeled "Pierre Leroi" are a chore to search by hand; their equivalent on a disk can be plucked out more quickly by the computer, but the printout can still be a long one. It helps to be able to specify "location: Canada" and get rid of the Belgians and French people.

In running traces, incidentally, the file clerk can do some selective purging as part of the maintenance function. I remember decades ago seeing a 3-by-5 card labeled "OPEL, Captain fnu" (fnu = "first name unknown") flagging a 1946 U.S. Army Counter Intelligence Corps (CIC) Germany report on something to do with an atrocity investigation. Unlike the person who carded that report, the amused file clerk who found the card happened to know that in 1946 the CIC was using many automobiles made· by Opel, which had the model named Kapitän. The CIC agent was merely recording what vehicle he had been using on surveillance. We destroyed the card, but not the report, which had some other, real names in it.

CASE FILES

In the field, keep all the information from and pertaining to a case you or your team are running in one folder or set of folders. The basic file, of course, is the case chrono, but if the case amounts to anything, you will want to copy or abstract portions from the chrono into other sections—for example, contact reports, surveillance reports, guidance/instructions, logistics/finance, and P-files (dossiers), which will contain all name traces and abstracts of biographic information on personalities (hence "P") in the case. In double agent cases you will have to have other sections: legend, requirements received, build-up cleared, build-up passed, build-up pending clearance, and so on. Most CI officers also keep a log labeled "running list" or "hold in despair" for reminders to themselves, random thoughts, and odd tidbits that don't quite fit the picture.

These are your working files in the field and those of your desk at the home office, where you get your support—that is, tracing, collation, and guidance. Obviously not all field situations permit the keeping and massage of elaborate files, but if the field officer can't have them with him, such files had better be kept at some backup office, nearby or back home, and he had better be in close touch with that office. Otherwise he will be merely skating figure eights on thin ice.

The system sounds complicated, and often is. It sounds time consuming, and often is. But with discipline and diligence, it saves time in the long run and prevents disasters.

Incorporation of all correspondence between field and headquarters is the job of headquarters. It goes first into the chrono file and is then indexed by name (see above), and then gets whatever collation (see below) is in order. The case file has a being of its own and must be preserved intact under the name or code name of the case. Future generations will benefit from studying the case file; future cases will be influenced by it; future discoveries will be made; future lives may be saved.

Every old CI officer has his favorite old cases. One of mine is the "trust" case in which the Russian intelligence chief Felix Dzerzinsky scuppered the British just after World War I (this story was told by the BBC TV series *Reilly: Master Spy*). The available files on this case are not perfect, but enough exist to provide a lesson (ignored a few times since) in how not to get scuppered.

DOSSIERS AND P-FILES

If you are a prominent person whose death will interest the public, your local newspaper has a file on you containing information the editor of the obituary page can use the morning after you die. Meanwhile it can be used for reference by reporters mentioning you even before you die. This file can be found in the newspaper's "morgue" alphabetically under your last name. In a CI organization, such a file is called a dossier. The word is from the French and originally meant a bundle of papers bulging like the hump on the back of Quasimodo, the Hunchback of Notre Dame (the French *dos* means "back").

If you are an American citizen, you probably have a Social Security number. If you pay income tax to the U.S. government, that number (if the Internal Revenue Service, or IRS, didn't garble it) is on the file in which IRS keeps all your yearly "returns" and all correspondence with you, if they haven't lost it. The only physical difference between the IRS file and the newspaper's is that the newspaper gets at it ("retrieves" it) alphabetically through your name, whereas IRS uses the number. Why? Because if your name is Bill Johnson, the IRS has 7,419,387 files on various Bill Johnsons. The IRS hopes, and so do you, that only one of them has *your* Social Security number.

So, in addition to the chrono and case files, your organization will maintain permanent dossiers on individual persons at its headquarters, and you will maintain temporary dossiers, P-files, in the field, containing what you need at the moment. Your P-file will contain traces from home, including possibly a copy of the entire headquarters dossier. It will also hold new material as you collect it from whatever source, and copies of this you must ship promptly home, remembering that headquarters is your rock and your fortress, whence cometh your help.

Dossiers normally contain unclassified and unindexed material in addition to documents that are more formally managed; examples: a newspaper account of the wedding of a person's daughter, an extract from a person's school or college yearbook, an extract from the published roster of a person's organization—items that contribute to biography, whether relevant to a current case or not. CI deals with people. Whatever helps a CI officer understand the people he deals with is useful to him. Never neglect overt sources. Read the newspapers. Remember that information in the press is at best only 40 percent accurate, but though it may not give you useful facts, it conveys *attitudes*. The context in which a person is mentioned often tells you more about her than what is alleged or stated. So get that piece into her dossier.

Are you violating a person's civil rights or privacy by maintaining a dossier with information not directly reflecting criminal or subversive actions? Believe it or not, some people think that you are. I remember a friendly argument with the editor of an American magazine that had vigorously *and legally* advocated opposition to official U.S. foreign policy. When, using the Freedom of Information Act process, he obtained a copy of the FBI dossier on himself, he was distressed to find that it contained copies of articles that he had published, the military service records of his relatives, and an extract from his college yearbook ("most likely to succeed"? "brightest"? "brashest"?). If the files of *Who's Who* or the morgue of the *New York Times* had contained (as they probably did) the same information, he would have felt flattered, not persecuted. I tried to explain to him that when the line advocated by his magazine appeared to correspond closely to that of the Soviet Union, the question logically arose in the minds of CI people whether his magazine might be funded by the Soviet or Czech intelligence services, and whether the material printed might have originated with a Soviet, Czech, or East German disinformation apparatus. The investigation that produced a dossier on him was aimed not at him but at the Soviet Union. If the investigation had produced evidence of secret contact between employees of his magazine and Communist Bloc intelligence officers, the investigators would have had a lead to an operation against a hostile service. In that case he might have had the opportunity to assist his government, if he so chose.

DOSSIER NUMBERS

Because your headquarters dossiers are numerous and hold many similar or identical names, they must have numbers. In practice this means that almost all personalities mentioned in CI reports should be given numbers, even though many or most will never have dossiers. Wasteful? No, numbers are cheap, especially to a computer, and they provide a convenient shorthand for other identifying data—place of birth, location, and so on.

The military services of most countries assign serial numbers to all personnel, and the old U.S. military system constructed its personnel dossiers by prefixing the serial number with "201." In CI work a similar system is normally used, with a prefix such as "1" for dossiers on individuals, "2" for target groups, "3" for target organizations (see chapter 17 on collation), "4" for administration of personnel, and so on. Numbers are assigned serially as an automatic part of the tracing process. Thus, when you cable from the field asking traces on Elmer Nudnik, born April 12, 1962, the reply will include a newly assigned number preceded by "1." All future reference to Nudnik will include this number, as will all indexing of that name.

Inevitably, several numbers will be assigned to the same individual, for reporting from the field is fragmentary, and the chaps in Tokyo may have a Nudnik with no date of birth, while the ones in Stockholm may have no address. It may occur also that Tokyo's Nudnik uses an alias in Stockholm, thus unwittingly acquiring himself two numbers. When such duplication is discovered, one number must be canceled and information from both files consolidated. So the six-digit system you set up last year to accommodate 999,999 numbers may have to be expanded to seven or eight digits. Your computer will hardly notice the added strain.

DOSSIERS AND PRIVACY

People do not like to have files kept on them. I don't like it, the editor cited above doesn't like it, and if you say you don't *mind* it, I'll prove you a liar with my polygraph machine. People value privacy. In the end, the only thing you really own is yourself, and the credit bureau, telephone company, or police force that keeps a record of your private acts is taking away from you some control of your most precious possession.

You don't believe in primitive magic, but you have to sympathize with the Navajo squaw who weaves a thread of light color across the boundary of the blanket so that her soul can escape. Those "primitive" people who do not like to be photographed because, to them, taking their picture is taking part of their own being are not so different from you and me.

To cherish our privacy is built into us. We're programmed that way. It's a biological matter. No wonder a cottage industry has sprung up in the press denouncing dossiers, wherever kept (except by news organs, of course). The biologically innate requirement for privacy is a fact that the CI officer runs into—bang. The CI officer is paid to be nosy, and the dossiers of a CI service violate people's privacy. There is no getting round it.

But, and alas, the world we overpopulate today is not the world our species evolved for several million generations to cope with. In the past couple of hundred generations, we have suddenly produced nations, associations, industries, unions, organizations, federations, and alliances. Adapted through evolution to live in small tribes and villages, we find ourselves living in huge cities and huge nations. Despite the craving—the compulsion—for privacy that sticks in our genes from a few thousand years ago, we have abolished privacy. Starting about five thousand years ago, we went forth and multiplied. Now we keep the craving, the inborn need for privacy, but politically and socially we can't afford it. Poor us. We'll never make it as ants.

Poor CI officer; your job is to violate privacy, and you won't make many friends in the process. Your dossiers will be resented, denounced, and deplored, and many regulations will be devised to whittle them away, to limit their content, to destroy them. Many journalistic careers will be built thereby, and not a few political careers, because readers and voters, like you and me, hate to have files kept on them.

You'll just have to persevere. Build your dossiers, but keep them out of the wrong hands. You have violated privacy at the beginning; respect it thereafter. Remember that you hold in those files what is most precious to your fellow human beings: the shape of their identities. Be very careful that your role is that of respectful custodian, not God.

THE COLLATION OF
COUNTERINTELLIGENCE

Raymond Rocca, the Rock, once coined the term "Highland Weaver" for a certain kind of counterintelligence analyst. The Rock is recognized throughout the profession for knowing as much about how to set up and use files as anybody, and he noted that the best tweed in the world is woven in the Highlands of Scotland by women using hand looms. Each batch of cloth is beautiful, indestructible, and unique—about enough for a tailor in London to make one beautiful, indestructible, and unique suit. If the customer next year wants an additional pair of plus-fours or a waistcoat to wear with the suit, he is out of luck. The Highland Weaver's next batch of cloth will be different.

There is a little Highland Weaver in every detective, including every CI analyst. I have a lot of Highland Weaver in me, and when I work on a case, I am the expert and I expect you to come to me and to my files about that case, not to some central system set up for just ordinary cases that do not require my superior expertise to understand. I keep this case file in my safe and in my personal computer and, like my counterpart weaving tweed in the Highlands, I own this piece of work. It is part of *me*.

To my shame, the result of my Highland Weaving is a case file with a set of folders and an internal index that cannot be incorporated into the main system. This situation was OK when collation had to be done by hand, with multiple card files, marginal scribblings, place marking of documents, and draft summaries on yellow pads. But the advent of the computer has changed all that. Now the analyst's work must mesh ("micro-computer software has to interface") with that of a colleague in the next office or across the river or on the other side of the world, and the work of both *should* fit with systems used by all the service's computers, including the mainframes that hold the central index and store the basic records.

Alas, though, Highland Weaving will persist even in the computer forest, not only by case analysts but by the designers of the big systems to which the analysts are supposed to conform. Examples: (1) "Systems compatibility" between, say, the British Home Office (MI-5) and the American FBI is not likely to be comfortable, though they work together closely; (2) within the FBI, the software used for both CI and work against organized crime will not satisfy either component, and Highland Weaverism will ensue.

Help stamp out Highland Weaverism! Well, anyway, help control it.

WHAT IS COLLATION?

Collation is (1) indexing by categories; (2) sorting by categories; (3) analysis. One category, but only one, is "name." A common example of a name index is your telephone directory, useful to get old Charlie's telephone number, but not much use if you are trying to find out the number of the fellow who lives next door to Charlie whose name you don't know. For the guy next door, you must have a category "street address."

How many categories do you have in a phone book, of which only "name" is useful for retrieval: "name," "street number," "telephone number." Four more—"city" and "state" are printed on the front of the book, together with "date of information" (the publication date). "Country" is taken for granted.

Here is an example of having to find the guy next door in a
CI case: Suppose your home base has told you that there is a
clandestine Czech radio somewhere within a 1-kilometer circle
drawn on a map of Oslo. Suppose, further, that you cannot seek
help from the Norwegian authorities in locating the safe house
where the radio is. And suppose that there are no reference
books available that list street addresses with the names of their
owners (actually, there are such books sold in many cities for the
use of advertisers, political parties, etc.). The Oslo phone book
will not help you much. You can go through it and pluck out all
the personal names preceding the names of the streets within
your circle. You can then trace all the personal names through
your central index. If you get no hits, you can then sort your list
by address and send out a surveillance team to record all the
addresses not on your list—presumably the ones that do not
have telephones. Then by all the tricks of undercover investigation, you can begin identifying persons at the addresses without
telephones and tracing them. Drudgery.

How much easier it would be if your headquarters had
already copied (by optical scanning) the telephone books of
Oslo and other cities and could sort on name, street address,
and telephone number. How much easier if your headquarters
had also indexed all reports on Czech spy cases not only by
name but also by address. Half the initial drudgery would
have been done by the computer before you ever heard of
the case.

CATEGORIES FOR COLLATION

Here are some of the categories that CI analysts collate.

Name

In collation, you are often working on persons whose names
you do not know or who are using aliases. "Name" is therefore

a category you seldom sort on, because you hope your sorting of other categories will reveal names.

Identifying Data

The purpose of a category on identifying data is to separate the many John Smiths and Bill Johnsons from each other. The most commonly used is "DPOB"—date and place of birth, which are the items shown in most passports. In the master file in the central computer, these take two fields, an easily sortable numeric one for date (270423 = April 23, 1927) and an alphabetic one (CAN Calgary). Because your collation system may have the categories "location" and "activity," "place of birth" can be listed in "location" and "born" entered under "activity."

Position

The category "position" is one not usually sorted on. It is necessary to give you a quick handle on the subject, and must have a separate field so that it will not interfere with sorting on the other categories. It often contains a person's occupation ("magazine editor," "code clerk") but may also designate an operational function, such as "safe house keeper."

Idiosyncrasy

The category "idiosyncrasy" is like that used by criminal police as "MO—modus operandi." Where does the safecracker habitually lay down his tools, to the right or left of the safe?

It also applies to outstanding scars or marks. I once identified a Soviet spymaster from the report of a double agent, who observed that his Russian handler—my opponent in the game where the agent was the pingpong ball—had three fingers tatooed "A," "H," and "R" written backward. In Russian this spells "Anya," the name of the wife of a first secretary in a Soviet Embassy. When shown a surveillance photo of the man whose wife was named Anya, a defector from the KGB remembered him as a former colleague in the First Chief Directorate, where, of course, he had a different name.

Does he smoke a pipe? Polish the instep of his or her shoes? Wear a wedding ring on left or right hand? Shift his fork from left to right hand (American style) when eating? Keep handkerchief in his sleeve? Eyeglasses? Carry a (what kind of) weapon? Go regularly to church, synagogue, mosque, pagoda? These might be his idiosyncrasies.

Date/Time

All data should be dated or they get lost in the files. If @Kusnetsov ("@" is a conventional abbreviation for "alias" or "aka = also known as") was in Athens on the 15th and @Petrov did not get there until the 20th, the two are not identical. If they were there on the same date, they may be the same fellow.

Sometimes—for example, with radio transmission schedules—the time of day is important. The computer collation column for date/time *in the master file* should therefore be ten characters wide; for example, "6602211403" = 2:03 p.m. on February 21, 1966; imperfect dates, for example, "6602 = February 1966, can be melded into the master file by a simple "if, then" macro that will fill in blanks from right to left with zeros. Thus, "6602" becomes "6602000000" for sorting purposes.

Location

When you have no name or only an alias to work with, you ask, "Who was in that place at that time?" And "Was X somewhere else at that time?" If your double met @Kusnetsov in Stockholm on April 20, can you get the airline manifests for the week before? If so, you can check the names on the manifests and the points of departure against the master list of identified Soviet case officers. If you find that Second Secretary Balkin, the GRU officer stationed in Helsinki, took a short leave in Stockholm that week, you may have acquired an oddly shaped piece for your picture puzzle: @Kusnetsov is "i/w" (identical with) Balkin.

Check the dossier on Balkin. Maybe you now know enough about him to arrange a quiet talk with him. Maybe he is having trouble with his wife. Maybe he is worried about having to go home at the end of his tour. *Maybe you can recruit him.* In any event, having identified him is another step toward the kind of *counterespionage* operation that CI always has as its final objective. You are earning your pay. But don't forget that Balkin may be using the same bag of tricks against you.

As with "date/time," the degree of precision needed for collating "location" varies. The master file in your central computer must accommodate as much detail as is necessary for the most complicated case, and so it will have separate fields for country, region (province, state, etc.), city, and street address. But in working with a particular case on your personal computer, you will often be concerned with only one or two. An investigation in which all the action occurs in Toronto may leave it to the computer to fill in "CAN" for Canada in the country field.

Activity

What happened? This can be coded; for example, "RV" = agent meeting; "FD" = filled dead drop; "PR" = presence noted; and so on. Or it can be a field long enough for a short phrase in clear text. Either way, a rigid uniformity is necessary if you intend to sort on this category. Your computer is too stupid to list all agent meetings if you name some of them "agent meeting" and others "rendezvous." This is an example of where the Highland Weaver in you must be brought to heel. (Of course, when the material is being transferred to the main system, a search-and-replace routine can help; but don't depend on it.) "Date/time" and "location," collated together, produce patterns.

Contacts

"Contacts" and "group" are interconnected and specialized. In some ways, they are the most important kinds of CI analysis, because they produce large patterns, whole orders of battle of your enemy. Unfortunately they also require immense amounts of analytical input to your system, and they take up huge chunks of your computer's memory.

"Contacts" should be a section of every dossier that figures in an active case. The simplest tool for compiling it is a computer spreadsheet, set up in sortable columns. The data are abstracted from the dossier in random order, for organizing and sorting by the spreadsheet software: name of subject, name of contact, date, location, and under "activity," type of contact. When sorted by name of subject and date, the first two entries in the column "name of contact" will be the subject's parents; the date will be the subject's date of birth, and the "type of contact" will be coded as "F" for "family." If your subject is a double agent, the last entry under "name of contact" may well be NU (name unknown), and the "type of contact" may be "RvE" for "operational meeting with enemy case officer."

The spreadsheet contact file on your subject is easy to collate with other contact files and with other records. Names in the "name of contact" column can be easily and mechanically traced, and contact files on each of them can be created if they do not already exist. Merging of a number of contact files and cross-collation (using a macro to shift names between columns) then produce a "group," to which you can assign a name—for example, "Balkin Complex"—and which you can then collate with other subjects or other groups. What emerges is a "pattern" that is larger than the sum of its parts and also, like a doughnut, displays its hole, where lie the things you do not know and did not know that you did not know. Obviously, if you sort that "NU" entry by "time" and "location" against the same categories in other files, you may be able to replace "NU" with a name already on record in another case.

As if by magic, sometimes this kind of collation produces a picture of a whole espionage apparatus. And sometimes it clearly shows that none is there, which results in time being saved.

Group

A simple kind of group, not without its uses for CI analysis, is "family." Saint Matthew lists the male progenitors in a direct line back from the stepfather of Jesus of Nazareth to the patriarch Abraham: "Abraham begat Isaac; and Isaac begat Jacob. . . . And [xx generations later] Matthan begat Jacob and Jacob begat Joseph, the husband of Mary, of whom was born Jesus. . . ." Here and there along the line, a female is mentioned, but women were not relevant to the saint's purpose. He did not need the computer that he did not have.

In Asian and Arab countries, the collation of family relationships will often uncover political and economic relationships as well as intelligence complexes. The intricacies of Filipino politics, for example, suddenly become more comprehensible when family groups are collated, and the strong points of the intelligence, security, and paramilitary groups become more visible.

Most groups on which you will construct files will be the product of collation on the other categories mentioned above. For ease of further collation, you can assign names to these groups that will be listed in the column "name of subject." Then when you sort on contacts, the name of the group will be shorthand for whole complexes and will reduce the bulk of your working file. If you are using dossier numbers in conjunction with names, your group numbers should be in a separate series; that is, start with a digit reserved for groups. Thus "1" may start all dossier numbers assigned to individuals, "2" all those assigned to groups, and "3" all those assigned to organizations (see below).

Organizations

Formal organizations with formal rosters are a type of group, but they are given a separate file because of the bulk of information available on them. Political parties, college fraternities, sewing clubs, intelligence services, professional associations, military units. . . . They number in the thousands, maybe millions. The basic files should be modeled on your P-files—personal dossiers. Most should be set up only when they directly support collation on other categories; most should be retired to archives or destroyed when no longer of timely use. Why? Because they are bulky and clutter your system. You should retain only those in which the information has been clandestinely acquired, as in the case of an intelligence service. A roster of a soccer team, for example, can always be quickly put together from public sources if needed in a future investigation, while a stolen list of secret members of a terrorist organization cannot. (Believe it or not, international soccer players make pretty good couriers, if you can get them to stop thinking solely with their feet.)

USING COMPUTERS

For computer technicians in the spy business, unemployment is not a looming peril. Computers are an essential tool in every part of the business. In A *Perfect Spy* (New York: Alfred A. Knopf, 1986), the British author who calls himself John le Carré gives an example. (Much of le Carré's fiction is fact, and much of what he appears to invent is authentic, with the exception of the term "mole" (for a penetration), which he sucked out of his thumb.) In the novel, an American CI officer in Vienna, trying to identify a Czech mole of the British Service, speaks of "the night hours spent in front of my computer while I typed my damned fingers off, feeding in acres of disconnected data. . . . Names and records of all Western intelligence officers past and present in Washington with access to the Czech target, whether central or peripheral consumers. . . . Names of all their contacts, details of their travel movements, behaviour patterns, sexual and recreational appetites. . . . Names of all Czech couriers, officials, legal and illegal travellers passing in and out of the United States, plus separately entered personal descriptions to counteract false passports. Dates and ostensible purpose of such journeys, frequency and duration of stay" (p. 239). Later, "with one touch of the button everything came together, continents merged, three journalists in their late fifties became a single Czech spy," and having now discovered the identity of the mole's Czech handler, he gets the mole, Pym: "Every American city visited by Petz-Hampel-Zaworski in 1981 and 1982 was visited by Pym on the same dates" (pp. 246 ff). So much for fiction that is more succinct, if not truer, than fact.

But the CI officer for whom the computer is a tool, whether in the field or at a home base, has to look at computers as if standing in Yellowstone or New Zealand at the edge of a geyser basin. The mud bubbles and burbles and throws up little burps or big eruptions of software and hardware that all seem to smell the same—slightly sulfurous. The one thing of which you can be certain is that whatever system you buy, it will be obsolete, by somebody's standard, in practically no time. Meanwhile you have work to do, and you are stuck with whatever equipment you already own. You are also stuck with whatever variety of equipment your various partners in the CI business are using, because inevitably you will want to trade information on CDs or online. The compatibility of both hardware and software between you and your partners in other services and in other offices of your own organization will either have to exist or be contrived.

If your CI service is a big one, it will have "mainframe computers"—the big guys in the air-conditioned cellars that hold (at minimum) all the CI records along with all the personnel records, the equipment inventories, the financial accountings, the budget projections, the external correspondence, the court records of your legal department, and a dozen other huge files. If your service is a conglomerate, like the American CIA, with missions beyond CI to collect intelligence by clandestine and overt methods, to produce finished intelligence, to conduct paramilitary operations and propaganda and covert political action, then the number of software systems used in your cluster of mainframes will be numerous, and communication among them will be a major chore for the technicians at your center and for their managers.

Your own computer chores will be with smaller machines—the personal computers and laptops. Just as in an earlier era—when a field case officer or investigator needed to be able to handle a typewriter, and fell back in his career if he could not type at least a draft of his reports—now an officer or investigator had better know how to handle a computer and had better know how to do the rudimentary collation of her own cases as well as the word processing that has replaced old-fashioned typing.

THE BIG GAME: DECEPTION

If you tell the communist Russian dictator that the Nazi German dictator is about to attack him, he will not believe you. The two have just made a sensible deal to carve up Europe between them, and why should the German give up all the advantages that the deal would produce, especially because he already has a big war going on in the West? "Hitler fight on two fronts?" asked Stalin. "Nonsense." But it happened, and the deal, called the Partition of Poland, turned out to be a German deception, which very nearly succeeded in turning Stalin into a German slave or a corpse dangling from a German gibbet.

If you tell a general who is waging a successful offensive that the enemy is withdrawing to prepared positions, he will believe you, because that is what he would do if he were the enemy. If you tell him that the enemy is preparing a counteroffensive, he will not believe you, because such a maneuver would be illogical and suicidal. So it happened in the Ardennes just before Christmas 1944. The German army, by all logic, was supposed to withdraw to the line of the Rhine but instead counterattacked. The Allied side, having refused to believe its intelligence, fell victim to the German deception plan. After the Battle of the Bulge was over, the Allied commanders found small consolation in the fact that indeed the Germans had just lost the war in the West. The German armies were in tatters, the way to Berlin was almost clear, but the snow-clogged roads of the battlefield were littered with Allied tanks and trucks and the fields of the Ardennes were littered with the bodies of Allied soldiers. The American and British casualties could have been prevented or reduced by a different deployment of troops before the battle started, one based on available intelligence.

During the Cold War, if you told a Western intelligence service that a communist government in Eastern Europe was being undermined by an internal resistance organization comprised of veterans of the country's formerly noncommunist army, it would have believed you, because it knew that the citizenry of that country was opposed to the communist regime. So it happened that the Polish State Security Service was able to deceive the American intelligence service and gain control, for a time, of Western espionage operations against Poland. They had modeled their operation, built around a fictional resistance organization called "WiN" (Wolnosc i Niedoplenosc—"Freedom and Independence"), on an older one ("The Trust") run against the British Service by the Russian Feliks Dzerzinskiy. Dzerzinskiy's OGPU (parent of the KGB) captured and doubled a member of the Monarchist Union of Central Russia (MUCR), a genuine anti-Bolshevik organization, and used him to recruit the head of MUCR, Boris Savinkov. Under Bolshevik control, Savinkov bamboozled Sidney Reilly and the British Secret Intelligence Service, which paid for Dzerzinskiy's operation by funding MUCR with millions of pounds sterling.

The more examples of such intelligence "failures" that one studies, the more one comes to think that failures to collect intelligence are vastly outnumbered by failures to read it. What is the moral of this? That decision makers believe what they want to believe, and the best way to deceive them is to feed them the intelligence that coincides with their preconceptions and their prejudices.

One qualification: The attitude toward intelligence in the former Soviet Bloc was different from that in the West. The

Soviets tended to believe what they stole through espionage more than what they got free in the press or in academic papers. In the West, particularly in the United States, the opposite was true. American intelligence analysts (and politicians, professors, and that contradiction in terms, "concerned scientists") would trust the *New York Times* more than a spy's report, and would often believe Soviet propaganda while discounting facts reported by clandestine sources.

Soviet deception (variously, *aktivnyye meropriyatiya, desinformatsia, maskirovka*) therefore played heavily toward the public media, while Western deception had to play toward the communist espionage services. Put simply, the Soviet deceivers contrived to get their stuff publicized in the West; we tried to get our stuff stolen by the Soviets and all the minion intelligence services of their empire.

THE TOOLS OF DECEPTION

The tools of *counterintelligence*, discussed throughout this book, are those that uncover and penetrate the enemy's intelligence—its collection, analysis, and estimates.

The tools of *deception* are those same tools of CI, used to manipulate the enemy's collection and thus distort its analysis and, later, its estimates. They are tactical, and because deception must be strategic, those using it must coordinate all the tools of CI and counterespionage, and these must be supported by all other available means. Let's examine the main techniques and aspects of deception.

Orchestration

Beethoven writing a symphony or Benny Goodman composing a swing arrangement used basic tunes that can be picked out with one finger on a piano. But a musician with a piano and one finger is not likely to fill a concert hall. The tune, or the deception theme, must be orchestrated. There must be fiddles and flutes and brass and percussion, and there must be a conductor firmly in charge.

Yesterday

If the Germans had believed that the Allies would assault the beaches of Normandy in the summer of 1944, they would have deployed their forces in such a way that the invading forces would have surely been destroyed. As it was, the Germans were fooled into believing that the main assault would come at the point nearest to England, the Pas de Calais. On FORTITUDE, which was the deception plan for Operation OVERLORD (the seaborn assault on the beaches of Normandy), hung the fate of the war. If FORTITUDE had failed, OVERLORD would have failed. Britain, France, and the United States would quite simply have lost the war, and your friendly author would not have survived to write this book.

The theme of FORTITUDE was simple: The Allies intended to invade Occupied France via the Pas de Calais. It was orchestrated by (1) defining every conceivable source from which German intelligence could acquire information, then (2) by controlling and manipulating those sources, and finally (3) by maintaining absolute secrecy about the plans for the real invasion.

Such orchestration required manipulation not only of the German spy apparatus but also of many other sources. The world press, with its speculative and often unscrupulous churning out of whatever "news" could be made to look new, was provided with "news." The most flamboyant general available, George Patton, was given command of First U.S. Army Group (FUSAG), with headquarters opposite the Pas de Calais; and the FUSAG was given a Signal Battalion (the 3303d) to simulate the massive radio traffic that an Army Group with dozens of divisions would generate as it prepared to smash across the Channel. Catering to German aerial reconnaissance, the few troops actually assigned to FUSAG built hundreds of dummy landing craft, hundreds of plywood tanks on jeep chassis, and hundreds of acres of camouflaged, empty bivouac areas. In Scotland the British Fourth Army was activated, with the II Corps based in Stirling and the VII Corps in Dundee—all shams.

German intelligence had twenty agents in Britain, a number coincidental with that of the XX Committee, which had doubled them all, though of course it couldn't be known for sure at the time that twenty was the total number. To guard against the agents that Allied CI had to presume were lurking undetected, the XX Committee leaked information about FUSAG and the British Fourth Army into the rumor mills. If in that gloomy winter of 1943–44 you had sat with me in a London pub, you would have heard FUSAG mentioned often, but the 12th Army Group (the actual top U.S. combat headquarters) practically never. You would have seen FUSAG commander Patton with his pearl-handled revolvers often going in and out of the American Embassy on Grosvenor Square, a cluster of reporters trailing after him, but you'd not have seen 12th Army Group commander Omar Bradley in public.

Of the twenty Abwehr agents controlled by the XX Committee, nine were radio agents, communicating with Abwehr stations on the mainland. In those days radio agents used manual "keys" to make signals in Morse Code. Each had his own rhythm, style, speed—what the communications people called his "fist," and operators grew to know each others' "fists" as they would the handwriting of a friend. So if you wanted to let your opponent know that your radio double was under your control, you got somebody else to send his messages, with a different fist. You could then insert a true item into the traffic, knowing that it would be disbelieved and would thus cast doubt on any similar true report from any enemy agent whom you had *not* uncovered.

Eleven of the XX Committee's double agents used secret ink through mail channels. Routinely, the Abwehr provided such agents with a "control signal," an inconspicuous mark to insert in their message indicating that they have been captured and were reporting under enemy control. A true item included in a message containing a control signal thus had the effect of discrediting the truth and reinforcing whatever deception the Allies were using elsewhere. "OBSERVED US 2 INF DIV MOVING FROM N. IRELAND TO S. WALES, REPLACING US 28 INF DIV," a true item sent with control signal in the spring of 1944, would have reinforced the deception that both the 2nd and 28th divisions were in Kent training for the assault on the Pas de Calais.

The British deception program in World War II, which Churchill called the "bodyguard of lies," was glorious, no doubt about it. To say with some historians that it won the war, saved Europe (including Germany, Austria, and Italy) from the cult madness of Naziism, is to rob glory from the thousands who bled, sweated, and wept, who fought and died without a thought of deception. Deception did not win the war, but it kept us from losing it. Would it be possible in today's world? Would it be possible against today's threat to Western civilization?

Probably not. The conditions that made orchestration possible in the British deception operations then do not prevail now and did not prevail during the Cold War, except among our enemies behind the Iron Curtain. During World War II, Britain was a sealed island, with all entry from the mainland controlled; it was then much like the Soviet Bloc—difficult to enter and, once inside, impossible for the entrant to evade official scrutiny. It was under strict central control, so that all actions of all inhabitants could be coordinated, again as in Eastern Europe and the Soviet Union during the Cold War. Finally, it had a unanimity of purpose throughout its population, properly called "patriotism." That patriotism and fortitude made it possible to endure the wartime dictatorship that made possible the success of FORTITUDE and the winning of the war. As soon as the war was safely won, the British people turned their elected dictator, Winston Churchill, out of office in a conventional peacetime election. Their finest hour had passed, and their beloved Winnie passed with it so that Britain could get back to being a democracy.

Today, patriotism is quite unfashionable in Britain, America, and the whole of the Western World. I sometimes ask those of my friends who write and teach history, "On what date did the land of the free cease to be the home of the brave?" They always change the subject, thinking, perhaps, that I live too much in the past, or in the future.

Today

Times are tough for CI, but deception remains the ultimate objective of CI, and deception must be orchestrated to succeed. So how, today, is orchestration accomplished? Let's look at the familiar example of the Soviet Union during the Cold War.

The Soviet government and its satellites used a huge, monolithic bureaucracy for the purpose. At the top sat the International Department of the Communist Party, directly under the supreme governing body, the Politburo, headed by the general secretary of the party. The general term used by the Soviets for deception was "Active Measures" (*aktivnyye meropriyatiya*) and included "disinformation" (*dezinformatsia*), camouflage (*maskirovka*), and activity that we would call black propaganda. The International Department formulated and coordinated (i.e., orchestrated) all "active measures," from the public activity of the secretary (who is chief of state, attends "summits," etc.) to the use of camouflage and dummy installations by, for example, an artillery unit on the Chinese border. Through the International Information Department, it controlled all internal media and all sources of information for foreign media. Most important, through four elements of the First Chief (foreign) Directorate and three of the Second Chief (domestic) Directorates of the KGB, it orchestrated all forms of deception used in CI operations. These included forgeries, information planted by agents of influence, and information passed through double agents, through provocation agents, and through false defectors.

As you see, the Soviets were organized to orchestrate deception.

We in the West are not so organized. We have pluralistic societies, pluralistic political systems, and pluralistic media. When Arnold Weber left the University of Colorado to become president of Northwestern University, somebody in Chicago asked him what Boulder, the site of his previous job, was like. "It's the only town I know that has its own foreign policy," he said. But he was wrong to think Boulder unique. In the United States any town, any group, or any individual is likely to have its own foreign policy, and if that comes in conflict with the official policy of the nation, too bad for the nation. Members of Congress quite routinely visit foreign countries where they use their positions in the legislative branch to disrupt the policies of the executive branch's Department of State. Factions within departments of the executive branch routinely leak to the press information on work of other factions with which they disagree. Components of the U.S. armed forces routinely use their huge public relations budgets to lobby for favorable funding, aircraft carriers over ground weapons, tanks over destroyers, jet bombers over submarine missiles, submarine missiles over reconnaissance satellites, and so on—all in full view of a bewildered public. Physicists in our universities turn politician and use the scientific journals to advocate partisan positions.

This pluralism is not limited to the United States. It prevails throughout the Western world, and on the whole it is pluralism that makes the Western world a better place to live in than countries without it, like China, North Korea, and Vietnam. But for the few specialists in CI work like you and me, it is a mixed blessing. It is not well adapted to the orchestrating of deception in foreign affairs, military affairs, or the spy business.

THE PRACTICAL LIMITS

During the Cold War, the Soviets had an awesome orchestra on which to play their strategic tunes, and what did we have? Only CI. We still do. So we must play CI tunes. Our audience is limited to our opponent's intelligence services. Our instruments are (1) provocations, (2) double agents, (3) penetrations, and (4) a support apparatus—a string quartet against the enemy's horns and kettle drums and squawking bassoons. But this limitation is not as crippling as it sounds. The essence of the Soviet system was conspiracy. Its intelligence services were its heart, lungs, and brain. To grapple with the KGB (or any of its brood of Satellite State Security and Military Intelligence Services) was to grip the Soviet System's windpipe. Because our system is not conspiratorial and doesn't much like to grip windpipes, our politicians, journalists, and peace-loving citizens hate to believe this obvious fact, but as a CI officer, you'd better believe it.

Objectives and Policy

Deception is an instrument of policy. It is not a bagful of pranks. Its objectives just be the objectives of your government. This means that it must be controlled by a bureaucratic mechanism that is an arm of your government's policy. If ever in the spy business there is a place where rogue elephants cannot be tolerated, it is deception.

("Rogue elephant," by the way, is a term coined by an American politician named Frank Church. He was an example of the kind of official to whom management of deception—or anything clandestine—must never be entrusted, for he lived in the world of journalistic publicity, a world where rogue elephants jostle each other for public attention; if ever there was a rogue elephant, it was Frank Church. He found the delightful china shop of "covert operations"—those nonclandestine activities that intelligence services perform, to the inevitable detriment of their clandestine work—and he smashed a lot of junky tableware along with some priceless porcelain. Being only a dumb bull elephant, he couldn't tell the difference, and he should not be blamed for the management's basic mistake, which was—in this counterespionage officer's opinion—to have put the good china into the same shop as the junk.)

One of the practical limits on deception, therefore, is the need for an organ—call it a committee or a staff—I'll call it a *Deception Board,* to formulate plans, review operations, and coordinate them. This is where the job of *orchestration,* mentioned above, is done. The board may be a single responsible officer (with plenty of clerical help), or a committee at the top echelon of your service, or an interagency committee, but it must report to and take decisions from your country's top policymakers. And it *must* include experienced, professional CI officers with clout. A Deception Board made up of amateurs will fail to deceive and will itself fall victim to deception. Enthusiastic amateurs often have brilliant ideas for deception, but when entrusted with the execution of their plans, they stumble and bark their shins, simply because without experience, patience, and skill, they cannot know where the furniture is in the darkness.

The Deception Board, like all bureaucratic devices, is a drag on the velocity of operations, but deception operations are best conducted without haste. The slower the board makes you work, the more time you have for attention to detail.

Objectives and Possibilities

The limits on our capacity for orchestration, as compared with that of the former Soviet Bloc, essentially restrict us to tactical methods. That is, because the only tools we can safely orchestrate are those of CI, our paths to our objectives must be through alien intelligence services. We cannot orchestrate our free press nor our freely elected legislators. We can, however, orchestrate our tactics to manipulate the enemy's operations and confuse its planning, using the tools mentioned below.

Executives of intelligence services are like all executives. They form their own opinions and sometimes disregard advice and ignore information from their staffs. They have their private views of how a foreign country, foreign government, and a foreign intelligence service work, and they base their decisions as much on that private view as on the papers they read and the briefings they hear. Further, their judgment is affected by their political environment. Unlike their subordinates, they are part of their country's political process, must constantly respond to their political bosses, and inevitably come to share political biases. Indeed, in some countries the intelligence executives are not intelligence officers at all but politicians or military flag-rankers appointed for their congeniality with their country's political leadership.

This situation is as common in the intelligence services of our enemies as it is in our own, and it constitutes precisely the same weakness for them as for us. Any intelligence service can be deceived more easily at the top than through the lower ranks because its leadership is prone to have preconceived beliefs that can be catered to and manipulated. Even in services headed by experienced officers—for example, the British Secret Intelligence Service and, occasionally, the American CIA—preconception plays a part in operational decisions. During the Cold War, an American officer experienced primarily in anti-Soviet operations would tend to read the Chinese as if they were Russian, and vice versa. On the other side, a Soviet chief who had built his career against the Americans in Europe would have goofed up his subordinates' work when they tangled with the Iranians or the Egyptians.

In many countries, especially those with one-man leadership, the man at the top often has his own intelligence apparatus of cronies that functions outside the structure of his government, independent of his intelligence service. Such leaders are especially vulnerable to deception, because the crony service is usually either amateur or off the main field of play; in either case the crony service lacks a support apparatus and a CI mechanism. It is easy to find, easy to contact, easy to bamboozle; and having the ear of the boss, it makes a lovely channel for deception.

THE RULE OF UNWITTING TOOLS

The tools of CI discussed throughout this book, when used for deception, are most efficient when the tools are themselves deceived.

Why is this unscrupulous rule a necessary one? Because if a messenger is coached to lie, he or she carries along with the message a burden of fear and guilt. He or she may slip up, or be forced by hostile interrogation to recant. How much simpler if he or she believes the message. For simple operational security, it follows that deception should begin with that messenger.

As a CI officer, you will have an ethical problem with this rule, or if you don't, you should. It goes against your principles, or should, to lie to a comrade in arms. And your messengers—the double agents, the provocations, the surveillance people, and the other support types—are your comrades. Even more painful is the realization that sometimes *you* are going to be the messenger, the boss who unwittingly passes on false messages to the messengers under your control. In fact, unless you are at the tip-top of the deception mechanism, it is only logical that the rule should apply to you also. This is the kind of ego-destructive situation that sometimes grows out of that first basic Rule of Need-to-Know.

Throughout this book, I have not been telling you that CI work is all tea with the vicar. If you can't accept the Rule of Need-to-Know and its corollary, the Rule of Unwitting Tools, better find another line of work.

Note, however, that the Rule of Unwitting Tools department is where the unreliable double agent, the agent known to have been turned against you, the habitual liar, and the sociopath can be put to use for deception. Wherever they have contact with the enemy, and you can be sure through independent sources that the contact really exists, you have a channel to the enemy. How you use it depends on your ingenuity. But don't simply play games. Use your ingenuity within the practical limits sketched above and orchestrate that ingenuity according to the objectives of your program.

Another form of Unwitting Tool is the technical one. The tapped telephone and the hidden microphone can both carry staged conversations, and the intercepted radio signal can carry contrived messages. Indeed, when you know that the enemy is intercepting some of your radio transmissions to agents, you can send traffic to agents that do not exist and set the enemy service to chasing phantoms. If (these days most unlikely) the enemy can decipher your messages, you can load the traffic with deceptive requirements or even suggest that some quite innocent enemy official is under your control.

THE SECRET BODY NEEDS
A BODYGUARD OF LIES

History, and the situation in the world in the dawn of the new century, tell us that clandestine intelligence is an intrinsic function of government, and that deception is an intrinsic function of clandestine intelligence. That is to say that no nation can long endure without intelligence about its enemies, its potential enemies, or its friends, and a critical part of that intelligence must be acquired by espionage. Espionage cannot function without CI, and an intrinsic element of CI is deception.

About the Author

William R. Johnson was born in Loveland, Colorado. He attended the Hotchkiss School in Connecticut and Yale University, from which he graduated in 1942 with a degree in English literature. During World War II he served as a combat intelligence officer with the U.S. Second Infantry Division from Omaha Beach (June 6, 1944) to Pilsen, Czechoslovakia, in 1945. Upon returning from the war he taught English at Carleton College in Minnesota and then joined CIA in 1948. As a young case officer he had several of the best coaches in the business of counterespionage, among them the Americans Jim Angleton, Bill Harvey, and Bill Hood. He was also coached by some British officers who cannot be named. He served twelve years in Austria and Germany before managing CIA's Far Eastern counterintelligence operations from 1960 until 1973. He was a senior command officer in the Saigon station until Vietnam fell in April 1975. He spent the last year of his service with CIA writing a classified counterintelligence training manual for young case officer recruits.

Johnson retired to his native Colorado in 1977, where he organized and managed a series of seminars and lectures on intelligence as a function of government that was part of the University of Colorado's annual Conference on World Affairs. *Thwarting Enemies at Home and Abroad* was first published by Stone Trail Press in 1987, after obtaining clearance from CIA. Johnson died in 2005.

Index

Quotation marks around entries denote specialized spy jargon.

"executive action" (arrest and prosecution), 15, 78, 98

Federal Bureau of Investigation (FBI)
the Central Intelligence Agency and, 16–19
MI5, information withheld from, 167
separation of prosecution from counterespionage within, 14
Felfe, Heinz, ix–x, 133, 137–39, 146
files
  bulkiness of, 176–77
  case, 179–80
  chronological, 175–76
  dossier numbers, 182–83
  dossiers and P-files, 180–82
  as essential to the counterintelligence officer, 175
  Highland Weaving's impact on, 185–86
  indexing by name, 177–79
  privacy and dossiers, 183–84
  target, 143–44
  See also collation
Fischer, William, 105
"flap," origin as American bureaucratic slang, 18
forgery shop, 23
FORTITUDE, 199–202
"freelance" agent, 91
"friendly" services, use of. *See* liaison

"game," 127
Gehlen, Richard, 138
gender, vulnerability to enemy recruitment and, 109–10
Germany
  counterintelligence activities, organization of agencies involved in, 13–14
  deceived by FORTITUDE in World War II, 199–202

deception by during World War II, 196–97
informants in Nazi, 112
intelligence service of the Federal Republic (*see* Bundesnachrichtendienst)
Soviet counterintelligence and Nazi, 129–30
Gilbert, Jean, 105
Gilbert, Otto Attilla, 98
Glavnoe Razvedovatel'noe Upravlenie (Soviet Military Intelligence Service, GRU)
  penetration of, Popov as, 92, 135, 141, 152, 166
  recall of agents by, 9
Goldfus, Emil R., 105
Goleniewski, Michal, 141, 150–51, 166–67
government employment, polygraph use and, 60–62
group, as category for collation, 192
GRU. *See* Glavnoe Razvedovatel'noe Upravlenie (Soviet Military Intelligence Service)
guilt conditioning, 50–51

hand signals by surveillance teams, 73–74
Harvey, Bill, 127
Highland Weaver, 185–86
Hitler, Adolf, ix
Hood, William, 92, 127, 135–36, 152
House, Edward Mandell ("Colonel"), 165
Hugo, Victor, 173
Hungarian State Security Service (AVH), 94–98, 128, 149

identifying data, as category for collation, 188